ALEXANDER CAMERON RUTHERFORD:
A Gentleman of Strathcona

Funding for this publication was provided by:

**THE EMIL SKARIN FUND
MRS. HAZEL McCUAIG
THE ALBERTA FOUNDATION FOR
THE LITERARY ARTS**

RUTHERFORD HOUSE 1912

ALEXANDER CAMERON RUTHERFORD:
A Gentleman of Strathcona

D.R. Babcock

The Friends of Rutherford House
and
The University of Calgary Press

ISBN 0-919813-57-7 Paper bound ed.
0-919813-65-8 Hard cover ed.

The University of Calgary Press
2500 University Drive N.W.
Calgary, Alberta, Canada T2N 1N4

Canadian Cataloguing in Publication Data

Babcock, Douglas R.
    Alexander Cameron Rutherford :
    A gentleman of Strathcona

    Includes bibliographical references.
    ISBN 0-919813-65-8
    (bound. --ISBN 0-919813-57-7) pbk.

    1. Rutherford, A. C. (Alexander Cameron),
1857-1941. 2. Alberta - Politics and
government - 1905-1921.* 3. Prime ministers -
Alberta - Biography. 4. Alberta - Biography.
I. Title.
FC3672.1.R88B32   1989   971.23'02'0924
F1078.R88B32   1989   C89-091452-4

Cover design by Rhae Ann Bromley

Printed in Canada

CONTENTS

LIST OF ILLUSTRATIONS

PREFACE

Alexander Cameron Rutherford (1857–1941) ranks among Alberta's most distinguished figures. He was the first premier of the province (1905–10) and the founder of the University of Alberta. His record of long and generous service to many organizations and institutions in Alberta is unsurpassed.

Rutherford epitomizes the public-spirited Ontario-born professionals who seized the opportunity to participate directly in the early development of the prairie West. His arrival in the new community of Edmonton South, District of Alberta, in 1895 coincided with the emergence in the West of the movement for provincial autonomy, a movement fostered largely by Ontario-born immigrants. As a product of Victorian Ontario whose cultural identity included Scottish, Baptist, and university affiliations and a successful career in law, Rutherford had the credentials to join the Ontario elite that already dominated the social and political life of the West.

Albeit reluctantly, Rutherford soon entered politics at the urging of his western friends. In 1902 he won election to the territorial legislature; three years later he became leader of the Alberta Liberal Association and, in quick succession, premier of the newly created Province of Alberta. As premier of a province whose lands and natural resources were controlled by the federal government, Rutherford quickly discovered frustrating limitations on his government's autonomy and ability to promote provincial development. His determination nevertheless to proceed with such provincial initiatives as the university, the telephone system, and northern railway development earned harsh criticism among influential Liberals in both Alberta and Ottawa. This, combined with Rutherford's non-partisan political style, eventually alienated him from the fiercely partisan Liberal establishment that forced his resignation in 1910 on the grounds of his involvement in an alleged railway scandal. Rutherford's political career ended with his defeat in the 1913 provincial election.

For a man who was not a "politician," Rutherford achieved high political prominence. In fact, his political career is studded with irony. Though his administration was based on policies of fiscal restraint and balanced budgets, subsequent governments faced crippling public debts incurred by Rutherford's administration. Though he and his administration were characterized by honesty, sobriety, and reliability, Rutherford was forced from office amidst allegations of corruption and irresponsibility. He was unseated at a time when his government overwhelmed the legislature and his personal popularity had soared. The railway guarantee policy that led to his downfall had, only a year earlier, brought him almost universal acclaim. Though he always considered himself "a true Liberal," Rutherford bitterly opposed such prominent Liberals as Frank Oliver and Arthur Sifton, and he campaigned actively on behalf of the Conservative party.

Rutherford's eleven years of active political life, however, provided a legacy for Alberta. He advocated provincial autonomy for Alberta before and after it was formed. As premier, provincial treasurer, and minister of education from 1905 to 1910, his touch dominates the province's founding legislation. His personal stamp is most evident in the educational and cultural institutions his government established: the public school system, the University of Alberta, the public libraries, the Historical Society of Alberta. Of these, the founding of the university was Rutherford's proudest achievement, although it cost him dearly in political terms—another irony. The railway crisis of 1910 left the Liberal party divided and the electorate disillusioned. Rutherford remained alienated from the Liberals, becoming one of the archetypes of western alienation.

Although an early political casualty, Rutherford nevertheless remained active in the legal, business, social, and religious institutions of his adopted province. He played a prominent part in such diverse organizations as the Alberta Historical Society, the Young Women's Christian Association, the Baptist church, and the Canadian Authors' Association. He remained the active senior partner in the law firm he had established in 1895 until his death in 1941. He was a member of the first senate of the University of Alberta and remained on the senate until 1927 when he was elected chancellor, a post he held until his death. Recognition of his contributions to higher education in Alberta came in the form of four honorary LL.D. degrees.

Because of his political and social status, and his extensive involvement in community activities, Rutherford's house became one of the major centres of social life in the Edmonton area even though Rutherford himself was inclined to be reserved and modest. Thrust into political prominence almost in spite of himself, he presided at the birth of a province and did not shrink from the duties entailed. Rutherford personified the work ethic, and quietly and unassumingly laboured to realize his vision of a decent, traditional society.

In 1966 the University of Alberta began an expansion programme eastward across 112 Street. In its path stood a residential neighbourhood that included a number of fine old homes. Among them was the fifty-five-year-old residence of Alberta's first premier and founder of the university, Alexander Cameron Rutherford. It seemed ironic at the time that his house should be doomed by the very institution he had established so proudly as minister of education, and served so well as university senator and chancellor. The irony was only heightened by the fact that the house had long been virtually an extension of the university and an integral part of its tradition.

Dr. Rutherford probably would have appreciated the irony in these developments, for the unexpected and contradictory were recurring themes in his life. Rutherford

House, for example, was originally conceived as a premier's home in 1909 when Rutherford was at the pinnacle of his political career. In fact, it never fulfilled that dream: Rutherford resigned his high office before the house was completed.

Thanks to public concern, the university did not engulf its founder's home. Restored to its original condition by Alberta Public Works and furnished by the Provincial Museum of Alberta, Rutherford House is operated as a museum and interpretive centre by the Historic Sites Service of Alberta Culture and Multiculturalism.

In April 1985 a group of individuals created the Friends of Rutherford House as a non-profit, charitable society, intended to assist in the preservation of the House and to enhance the cultural and recreational activities of the visiting public. By 1989 the Friends society had over one hundred active members participating in its many activities.

The Friends organization has sponsored many special events at Rutherford House, including a Croquet Challenge every June and Achnacarry each August. In addition to the many programmes offered by Alberta Culture and Multiculturalism, the Friends opened a Tea Room and gift shop and operate a historic children's programme every summer. The society published a children's activity book just before producing this book.

This study of Alberta's first premier had its beginning in 1974 in a modest assignment to prepare a brochure for distribution to visitors at Rutherford House. The original brochure betrayed how little we knew of Dr. Rutherford at that time: it merely touched on highlights of his life and revealed little about the architectural significance of his 1911 home. But as more information came to light, the brochure evolved. Meanwhile, another need was identified: the interpretive staff at Rutherford House required a reference book that would help them to answer the many questions posed by visitors about the Rutherfords, their home and their times. This assignment launched a lengthy research process that led to the production of an Occasional Paper on Rutherford by the Historic Sites Service, Alberta Culture and Multiculturalism. The search had been both rewarding and disappointing. The principal reward came in the form of numerous interviews with Mrs. Hazel McCuaig, Rutherford's daughter, who remembered so much and generously shared it. But written sources were scattered and often limited. For example, the Rutherford Papers at the University of Alberta Archives provided little that had not been reported in the daily newspapers, and the newspapers, once Rutherford left politics, focussed mainly on the Rutherfords' roles in the social life of Edmonton. Subsequent revisions addressed the lack of social and political context to some degree and developed Rutherford's experience with the western Canadian theme of alienation.

The search for the historical Alexander Cameron Rutherford has been long and checkered, yet still not conclusive. This new edition of *A Gentleman of Strathcona* is a report on progress to date, along with some discussion of Rutherford's house,

Achnacarry. Both the book and the house emphasize Rutherford's personal link with the institution most dear to him, the University of Alberta, and connect us with Alberta's origins.

ACKNOWLEDGEMENTS

The writer gratefully acknowledges the valuable assistance of several people during the preparation of this book. Without the generous help of Mrs. Hazel McCuaig, Dr. Rutherford's daughter, the research task would have been much less rewarding. In addition to providing several interviews and answers to interminable questions, Mrs. McCuaig made available her own archives, consisting of family records, photographs, and newspaper clippings. The writer is also indebted to her for helpful comments on the original draft of this book. Mrs. Helen Rutherford kindly answered many questions about the Rutherford family and shared her historical photographs. Her recollections and written record of life in Rutherford House during World War I were especially helpful. Both Mrs. McCuaig and Mrs. Rutherford conducted Lorri Storr, former chief guide at Rutherford House, and the writer on a tour of the house, during which many interesting details about the building and its furnishings came to light. Bob Anderson, restoration architect for Rutherford House, revealed a wealth of detail on the structure of the house and the restoration process. Mrs. Lila Fahlman vividly recalled the Rutherford House controversy and provided a great deal of useful documentation. D. B. McDougall, Legislature librarian, made numerous sources of information available, and was particularly helpful in the search for the painter of the Rutherford portrait that hangs in the Legislative Building. Lily Roberge painstainkingly researched a forest of Alberta Supreme Court cases in the *Alberta Law Reports*, the *Dominion Law Reports* and the *Western Weekly Reports*. Graham McDonald researched the early issues of the *Kemptville Advance*. Patricia Myers ruthlessly and thoughtfully edited the original text and made numerous helpful suggestions. The staff at the University of Alberta Archives, the Glenbow-Alberta Institute, and the Legislature Library were invariably interested and helpful.

The Friends of Rutherford House wish to acknowledge the many volunteer hours the following individuals contributed to the preparations leading to publication of this book: Lori Becker, Jane Fullerton, John Lipinski, Sheila Petersen and Lori Stewart.

CHAPTER I

FROM CANADA WEST TO WESTERN CANADA (1857–1905)

In 1855 James Rutherford, his wife Elizabeth (née Cameron), and their four children[1] emigrated from their native Aberfeldy, Perth, Scotland, and settled on a dairy farm a few miles south of Ottawa near the village of Ormond, Carleton County, Canada West. The Rutherfords had been Congregationalists in Scotland and like many of the other Scottish settlers in the area, they became members of the Baptist Church, the nearest equivalent.[2] James Rutherford became a Liberal in politics and took a keen interest in agriculture and education. He served for a number of years on the municipal council of the nearby Village of Osgoode.[3]

It was on this family farm that Alexander Cameron Rutherford was born on 2 February 1857. Here he grew up, nurtured by the strong Scottish and Baptist influences of his family and neighbourhood. After attending the local public school, young Rutherford went to high school in nearby Metcalfe, having decided not to make a career of dairy farming. In 1874 he enrolled in the Canadian Literary Institute (C.L.I.) at Woodstock, a Baptist college southwest of Hamilton.[4] Some thirty years later his own son would enroll at the same institution, by then called Woodstock College.

Following his graduation from C.L.I., Rutherford taught school for a year in Osgoode. In 1877 he entered McGill University in Montreal and graduated in 1881 with degrees in arts and civil law. During the next four years Rutherford articled with the Ottawa firm of Scott, McTavish and McCracken and briefly with the firm of O'Connor and Hogg. Almost half a century later he fondly recalled this period of his life:

Figure 1: A. C. Rutherford, B. A., B. C. L.,
McGill University, 1881.
(Mrs. Hazel McCuaig)

Figure 2: A. C. Rutherford,
student-at-law, c. 1883.
(Mrs. Hazel McCuaig)

Figure 3: Alexander Cameron
(right)   Rutherford and Mattie
          Birkett on their
          wedding day, 19
          December 1888.
          (Mrs. Hazel McCuaig)

Figure 4: The Rutherford family at home, Kemptville, Ontario, c. 1893. Left to
(below)   right: Mattie, Hazel, Christie McNab (Rutherford's niece), Cecil, and
          Alexander Rutherford.
          (Mrs. Hazel McCuaig)

We were articled out and all our study was in the lawyer's office to which we were attached. There were no law schools. Some of my best days were spent in Ottawa under the guidance of Sir Richard Scott, afterwards Secretary of State for Canada in the first Laurier cabinet formed after the 1896 election. I imbibed much knowledge from this astute lawyer and statesman.[5]

In 1885 twenty-eight-year-old Rutherford was called to the Ontario bar and became the junior partner in the law firm of Hodgins, Kidd and Rutherford, of Ottawa and Kemptville.[6] For the next ten years he was in charge of the Kemptville office fifty-five kilometers south of Ottawa.[7]

Rutherford's social circle in Ottawa came to include W. C. Edwards, a prominent lumber merchant and later senator. Through Edwards, Rutherford was introduced to Miles Birkett, a member of another prominent family that included Thomas Birkett, a former member of Parliament.[8] His niece, Mattie Birkett,[9] was the daughter of William and Elizabeth Birkett. In December 1888 the thirty-one-year-old Rutherford and Mattie Birkett, eight years his junior, were married. Their first two children were born in Kemptville, Cecil Alexander Cameron Rutherford in 1890[10] and Hazel Elizabeth Rutherford in 1893.

During the summer of 1894,[11] perhaps intrigued by the federal government's promotional literature on the opportunities in the opening Canadian West, Rutherford travelled across the prairies on the Canadian Pacific Railway. From Calgary he took the C.P.R.'s Calgary & Edmonton Railway (C. & E.) north to its terminus on the south bank of the North Saskatchewan River, a community then known as South Edmonton. South Edmonton was in its raw infancy, having come into being only three years earlier when the C. & E. Railway was completed. On the opposite bank stood Fort Edmonton, the Hudson's Bay Company post and depot, around which the older and larger Edmonton settlement was taking shape.

The *Edmonton Bulletin* of 2 August 1894 reported that "A. C. Rutherford, an Ottawa lawyer, is in town and very much likes the appearance of the town and district." The "appearance," especially of South Edmonton, undoubtedly included the potential for growth and development. Located in fertile parkland at the terminus of a new railway, it was certain to grow rapidly as a service centre, thereby creating a sustained demand for land, capital, and the services of a lawyer. For Rutherford, there was business and professional opportunity for the taking, together with the compelling opportunity to participate in the transformation of a frontier settlement into a new metropolitan centre that would reflect the best of British Protestant Canadianism. A new and better Ontario could be built here and he could contribute. There was even a bonus: Rutherford suffered from bronchitis at this time and happily discovered that the climate in the West relieved his condition.[12] All things considered, he decided to settle in South Edmonton and did so ten months later.

Leaving Kemptville nevertheless could not have been easy, particularly for Mattie Rutherford. Her family lived in nearby Ottawa and the prospect of removing three thousand kilometers from familiar surroundings to a raw frontier she had never seen must have been intimidating. Rutherford had become a prominent and respected figure in the community, active in numerous organizations including the Masons, the Foresters, the Ancient Order of United Workmen, and the Kemptville Baptist Church in which he was an officer and President of the Young People's Union.[13] His law practice and business transactions had brought him status and affluence, reflected in his comfortable Kemptville home. His professional advertisement was still appearing daily in the *Kemptville Advance* when he and his family left Kemptville on 1 June 1895:

Kidd and Rutherford
Barristers and Solicitors etc.
Money to lend and borrow at
low rates of interest
Kemptville, Ont.
F. J. French   A. C. Rutherford

The editor of the *South Edmonton News*, himself a native of Ontario, noted that

two copies of the *Kemptville Advance* [contain] about a dozen addresses and presentations from the various Lodges to Mr. A. C. Rutherford. . . . They speak in highest praise of Mr. Rutherford and much regret his departure from their midst.[14]

Referring to his years at Kemptville, Rutherford would later comment that he had taken only a passing interest in politics, having "electioneered a little in the east."[15]

On 10 June 1895 the C. & E. Railway train pulled into the terminal station at South Edmonton, bringing Rutherford, his wife Mattie, their children Cecil and Hazel, and a carload of their furnishings to their destination.[16] Compared with the built-up capital area of Ontario, South Edmonton must have appeared unfinished and insignificant; Rutherford later remembered it as a settlement of only two hundred people in 1895.[17]

In fact, the North-West Mounted Police had enumerated 792 people there in November 1894, and just over a thousand across the river at Edmonton.[18] In any case, the community was growing and would be incorporated as the Town of Strathcona in 1899. Already a business section was rising in the vicinity of the railway station, around the intersection of Whyte Avenue and Main (later 104) Street. There were three hotels; general, hardware, and grocery stores; butcher and blacksmith shops; a flour mill; a business block (Parrish's); and the "inevitable" Chinese laundry.[19] South Edmonton's first bank opened in January 1895, and the few professionals in the community included only one lawyer, Mervyn Mackenzie, who left for Toronto in 1896. For Rutherford, the lack of legal service at the railhead was probably a factor in his decision to establish at South Edmonton rather than Edmonton proper.[20] Already too, the settlement had two public schools and four churches, including a Baptist church into which Rutherford was received in November 1895. Mattie Rutherford was a Methodist and, while she attended the Baptist church with her husband, she did not become a member.

The Rutherfords were participants in a great migration of people into the Canadian West that began slowly in the three decades following 1870, the year in which Canada acquired the Northwest Territories, but which greatly accelerated and diversified just after the Rutherfords' arrival in the West. The Canadian government's vision of the nation was that of a British state composed of an industrialized central Canada linked to an agricultural west by a transcontinental railway.[21] With its control of the immense lands and resources of the Territories, the central government could stimulate the necessary settlement and railway construction that would bring the vision to fruition. Virtually free land under the homestead policy would attract settlers in the thousands, while the C.P.R. would facilitate their arrival and the marketing of their wheat and livestock. And government promotion of immigration in central Canada, the British Isles, northern Europe, and the United States guaranteed the development of a British West. By 1891 the population of the District of Alberta was 25,000, almost equally divided between native and immigrant residents. Of the latter group, 81 per cent were British subjects, including 4,000 from the British Isles and over 7,000 from Canada. Included in the Canadian group were almost 4,500 Ontarians who constituted no less than a third of the total immigrant population. During the following decade (1891–1901) the population of the District increased to 65,000. The number of immigrants from continental Europe and the U.S. increased sharply, but British subjects retained their numerical majority. Of these, the Ontario-born remained a significant group—still one-quarter of the total immigrant population.[22]

British immigrants in the District of Alberta at the end of the century were not only numerically dominant:

> Unlike the European immigrants . . . they did not have to acquire citizenship and familiarity with the language and constitution before participating in public life. There were well-educated and well-to-do men among them, and all of them had a lively interest in politics.[23]

This appears to have been true of Ontarians in particular. Of the twenty-five members elected to the first legislature of Alberta in 1905, nineteen, including Rutherford, were Ontario-born, and two-thirds of the forty-one members elected to the second assembly in 1909 were Ontarians.[24] Natives of Ontario such as Rutherford were apparently ideal colonizers who would implement the federal government's vision of a British nation from sea to sea. As the personification of the values and virtues of British Canadianism, they would build a new Ontario in the Canadian West. This would take time, however, and the West was still Canada's colony, administered by Ottawa.

Figure 5:   Alexander Cameron
(right)   Rutherford, c. 1895.
             (Mrs. Hazel McCuaig)

Figure 6:   The Rutherford House at
(below)   8715 - 104 Street, c. 1900.
             (City of Edmonton Archives,
             EA-82-5)

How long would British subjects endure this colonial status? As early as the 1880s immigrant westerners were advocating provincial autonomy for the west. The *Regina Leader* in 1887 had warned that

> [t]he north-West is being settled by a liberty-loving people, educated in self-government, who will be satisfied with nothing short of an administration responsible to the people in the fullest sense of the word. And if any makeshift is given, it will invite agitation and lead to an early struggle for the rights and privileges enjoyed by the provinces.[25]

Four years later, in a scathing assessment of the territorial administration, the *Calgary Herald* asserted that "not a Canadian citizen in the east would submit to such government for a single moment."[26] By 1895 the autonomy movement was gaining momentum, fuelled by editorials in the *Calgary Herald*, public meetings, and the distribution of a pamphlet entitled *Provincial Government for Alberta. Its Meaning and Necessity.*

> The British subject who leaves the settled haunts of civilization and goes forth to open up fresh tracts and add new provinces to the empire, never imagines for a moment that in doing so he is relinquishing one jot or tittle of this right. For a while the necessities of the situation may lead him to acquiesce in a more irresponsible form of government than that to which he has been accustomed, but he regards this state of things as merely temporary, and looks with certainty to the time when every privilege of British citizenship will be handed to him unimpaired.[27]

It was in the midst of this ferment that Rutherford and his family arrived from Ontario with their material and cultural baggage. They would soon be caught up in that ferment.

Rutherford lost no time in getting established. Starting with a temporary base at the Raymond Hotel, he had, within ten days of arrival, opened an office in the Parrish Block, purchased four adjoining town lots on the east side of Main Street north of Whyte Avenue, and contracted Hugh McCurdy to build him a house there.[28]

During the fourth week of July the Rutherford family moved themselves and their furnishings and effects into the newly completed frame house. It was a modest one-storey home of four rooms and an attached kitchen,[29] but as Rutherford grew in stature in the community, so did his house. In 1899 he added a second storey containing four bedrooms. By 1905, when he became premier of Alberta, the second storey had been enlarged with three additional rooms, one of which was a maid's room.[30] Five years later a mansion, more in keeping with Rutherford's public prominence, was under construction near the site of the university.

Figure 7: Library of the Rutherford House at 8715 - 104 Street, c. 1906. (City of Edmonton Archives, EA-82-2)

Figure 8: Parlour of the Rutherford House at 8715 - 104 Street, c. 1906. (City of Edmonton Archives, EA-82-3)

On 11 October 1895, only four months after his arrival, Rutherford attended a meeting to organize the South Edmonton Football Club.[31] The meeting elected Rutherford honorary president, and this marked the beginning of what was to be his long involvement with an astonishing variety of voluntary associations in South Edmonton. He had already demonstrated his public spiritedness in the settled community of Kemptville, Ontario: the western settlement frontier provided even greater need and scope for it. In 1896 he became secretary-treasurer of the South Edmonton School Board and president of the South Edmonton Athletic Association. The following year he was vice-president of the South Edmonton Literary Institute, auditor of the South Edmonton Agricultural Society, and worthy master of Acacia Lodge, Ancient Free and Accepted Masons. He was secretary of the Edmonton District Butter and Cheese Manufacturing Association in 1899. In addition he often judged the numerous elocutionary contests sponsored by the Royal Templars of Temperance. In 1898, when meetings were held to discuss the incorporation of South Edmonton as a town, Rutherford chaired them.[32] In 1899 he was the advocate in the application for incorporation, and when the first elections for a mayor and council for the Town of Strathcona were held, Rutherford was chairman of the nomination meeting and returning officer on election day. At the first council meeting, held on 27 June 1899, the Council appointed Rutherford secretary-treasurer and legal advisor of the town,[33] a position he held until he became premier.

In June 1896 Frank Oliver, member of the Legislative Assembly of the Northwest Territories for Edmonton, was elected to the House of Commons and a by-election was called to fill the vacancy in the territorial assembly. Although he had been in the West for scarcely a year, Rutherford was urged by many individuals in the South Edmonton district to contest the seat, but he always declined. When a petition bearing three hundred signatures was presented to him,[34] however, he reluctantly accepted the nomination. Unable to reject such a clear expression of public confidence, Rutherford nevertheless felt intimidated by the prospect of entering politics. He campaigned against Matthew McCauley, who had been Edmonton's first mayor in the early 1890s, and who now eagerly sought the seat. Though the demand for provincial autonomy was gaining momentum and Rutherford had addressed a public meeting at Clover Bar on the subject in the spring, he appears not to have campaigned on that issue in the summer of 1896. Rather, he went to the people advocating resource development, improved roads, higher school maintenance grants, and the simplification of ordinances and court procedures. He concluded his election address in a characteristic way: "Should you favour me with your votes and influence, I shall do my utmost to merit your confidence. Your Obedient Servant, A. C. Rutherford."[35] McCauley won the by-election, but Rutherford picked up a respectable 40 per cent of the vote.[36]

In the fall of 1898, again at popular urging, Rutherford reluctantly sought election to the territorial assembly in the Edmonton electoral district. Once more his main opponent was Matthew McCauley. A third contestant, H. H. Robertson, would lose his deposit. Rutherford campaigned more vigorously than he had in 1896; his platform was based on independent support of the Haultain administration. F. W. G. Haultain,

Figure 9:   The Rutherford family on a picnic, 1897.
            Cecil at extreme left, Mr. and Mrs. Rutherford and Hazel grouped third
            from right.
            (Glenbow-Alberta Institute, NA-545-3)

Figure 10: Hazel Rutherford, c. 1900
Photo by C.E. Tighe, Strathcona, Alta.
(Mrs. Hazel McCuaig)

Figure 11: The Rutherford family, 17 December 1898.
(Provincial Archives of Alberta, B.10159)

premier of the Northwest Territories, was pledged to non-partisan government in the Territories, and the immediate elevation of the provisional districts of Alberta, Athabasca, Saskatchewan, and Assiniboia to the status of one province with the same degree of autonomy as existing provinces. At a political meeting in Edmonton on 13 October 1898, Rutherford detailed his platform at considerable length: better local roads; increased representation for the Edmonton district, on the ground that the present electoral district was a gerrymander for McCauley; the creation of a single western province after the 1901 census; and removal of the tax exemption on railways. He attacked McCauley's lacklustre record in the assembly and his silence on many issues affecting the Edmonton district.[37]

In the 28 October issue of the *Alberta Plaindealer* (formerly the *South Edmonton News*) Rutherford publicly challenged McCauley:

> I am informed that Mr. M. McCauley has stated in his canvass that I used the expression with regard to him "He's only a teamster anyway." If M. McCauley can produce anyone who can truthfully say that I ever said so I am willing to pay over $50.00 to the Edmonton General Hospital.

With his solid support in Edmonton, McCauley again defeated Rutherford, but by the narrow margin of eighty-four votes.[38]

Rutherford meanwhile carried on his legal practice from his office in the Parrish Block. At a time when the clerical work force was still overwhelmingly male, Rutherford employed single women to do his secretarial work. His original secretary, Miss Beulah Heath, was replaced in November 1897 by Miss Postle, who remained with him until 1902. In January 1897 Rutherford undertook the brokerage work that resulted from the establishment of a new customs office.[39] As a private attorney, he defended, usually with success, people charged with offences such as stealing oats, setting prairie fires, cattle stealing, stabbing, abduction, and indecent assault. He often received payment from his clients in the form of wool and coal, or butter and eggs. In March 1898 he defended an Indian named Crazy Calf charged with the murder of his wife. A wretchedly ill woman, she had died after being beaten. Rutherford's defence reduced the charge to assault causing bodily harm and Crazy Calf, found guilty, served a nominal sentence of three months at the Fort Saskatchewan North-West Mounted Police post.[40] Rutherford's daughter Hazel later observed that her father had taken this case at a time when few lawyers would defend an Indian in court.[41] In May of 1898 Rutherford became solicitor for the Imperial Bank of Canada and, a year later, solicitor for the new Town of Strathcona. In August 1899 he formed a partnership with Frederick C. Jamieson.[42] Jamieson supported Rutherford in the 1902 elections, but after the introduction of party lines in Alberta in 1905, the partners found themselves in competing camps, Jamieson being a loyal Conservative.

During the early days of the South Edmonton Literary Institute, of which he was vice-president, Rutherford was joined by J. W. Blain for the affirmative in a debate on the resolution that capital punishment be abolished. We may take this as an indication of Rutherford's position on this vexing issue; unfortunately, he and his partner narrowly lost the debate.[43]

Soon after his arrival in South Edmonton, Rutherford invested heavily in property. By the summer of 1896 he was running a regular advertisement in the *News*: "For Sale, Several improved and unimproved farms. Also South Edmonton Town Lots. Apply to A. C. Rutherford." In an 1898 editorial promoting Rutherford for M.L.A., the editor of the *South Edmonton News* stated that Rutherford's property investments were "not merely for speculation but for the country's benefit." They included valuable farm land just east of the town with seventy acres (twenty-eight hectares) under cultivation, as well as his investment in gold-mining equipment on the North Saskatchewan River.[44] His interests included an experimental plot of Red Fife wheat on his farm. From three pounds of seed planted in the spring of 1899, he harvested two bushels of No. 1 hard grain.[45] In that same year, Rutherford had a two-storey frame building erected on the southwest corner of Whyte Avenue and Main Street, the Rutherford Block.

By the turn of the century, Alexander Cameron Rutherford had become a prominent citizen in the town and district of Strathcona, successful in both his legal practice and his business investments. His integrity and sound judgement were universally recognized, as well as his willingness to serve in the many voluntary community organizations that shaped the social life of early Strathcona. Although political power still eluded him—he had not ambitiously sought it—he was nevertheless a figure of considerable personal influence in the district. Deeply involved in the political, social, and economic affairs of the time, Rutherford was soon to convert that influence into political power.

The demands of his legal practice, business affairs, and community involvements did not leave him much time or energy for his family. In 1896 Mrs. Rutherford took the children to Ottawa for a five-month visit. In the years to come she and the children would make numerous trips to Ontario: her father in Ottawa provided the return train fare whenever she cared to go.[46] Rutherford himself did not return to his native province until 1899 when he and his son Cecil spent Christmas at his old home in Kemptville.[47] Through the years both Rutherford and his wife maintained close contact with their respective families, and the local newspapers chronicled the comings and goings of eastern relatives, as well as the Rutherfords' periodic visits to Ontario.

By the summer of 1900 preparations were afoot for a federal election expected in the fall. In August the Liberals of the Town of Strathcona met to reorganize their association. They elected Rutherford president, and later that month he was a delegate to the Liberal convention that nominated Frank Oliver for re-election in the District of Alberta. On 5 November Rutherford chaired Oliver's campaign meeting in Strathcona and on 7 November Oliver was re-elected to the House of Commons.

Figure 12:   The Rutherford family, c. 1905
              (Mrs. Hazel McCuaig)

In the spring of 1902 Rutherford, now forty-five and seasoned by seventeen years of legal practice, finally embarked on a political career destined to be meteoric and productive, but ultimately tragic. Spectacular population growth in the Northwest Territories had led to redistribution of the territorial electoral districts, and in the new district of Strathcona Rutherford was again widely urged to stand for election to the territorial assembly. In Strathcona and throughout the West, the rapidly growing population pressed demands for provincial status with renewed vigour. On 5 May 1902 Rutherford was nominated by acclamation as an independent candidate for the territorial district of Strathcona; three days later he presented his platform at a public meeting in the town. Once again, he stood for independent support of the Haultain administration; immediate provincial autonomy; two provinces rather than one ("one province would be too large to be properly and economically governed") with all the rights enjoyed by the established provinces; more money for roads, bridges, and school maintenance; and removal of the tax exemption on such corporations as the C.P.R.[48]

Immediately after the meeting Nelson D. Mills, a Strathcona lawyer, wrote an open letter to Rutherford accusing him of being a Haultain supporter "pure and simple," after having posed as an independent candidate. Mills concluded by announcing his intention to contest the election as an independent, in opposition to Rutherford.[49] Rutherford replied to the "pure invention on Mr. Mills' part" with a reaffirmation of his position:

> Allow me to repeat that I am running as an Independent candidate and do not pledge my support to either the Government or the Opposition, but will act always for what I believe to be the best interests of the Strathcona District and the Territories at large.[50]

Strathcona was to have an election campaign after all. The campaign was fought at public meetings in Strathcona and in the school houses in Clover Bar, White Mud, Agricola, and Colchester. On the stump, Rutherford was supported by his partner Fred Jamieson, by Mayor Duggan of Strathcona, and by a young lawyer named J. R. Boyle who had established a law practice in Strathcona three years earlier. When the ballots were counted, Rutherford had won 571 to 67.[51]

At the legislative sessions held in Regina in 1903 and 1904, Rutherford ably represented Strathcona by sponsoring legislation that extended the town's boundaries and empowered it to borrow money for public works.[52] In addition, he was elected deputy speaker of the house. It was therefore his task to chair the assembly when it went into committee of the whole for the painstaking consideration of each bill following second reading, and then to report on the committee's progress to the Speaker when he resumed his chair. Rutherford remained deputy speaker until the final dissolution of the territorial assembly in 1905. Moreover, he served on such select standing committees as those for library, municipal law, and education, committees that accurately reflected his interests and abilities. Rutherford was also mentioned as a possible commissioner of public works in Premier Haultain's cabinet,[53] but the portfolio went instead to George Bulyea, who would later play a significant part in Rutherford's political career.

By 1903 the *Plaindealer* was referring to Rutherford as a Liberal in politics. There was at this time a consensus that party lines had no place in territorial affairs, a position championed by Premier Haultain. But as the era of territorial status drew to a close, more and more Liberals and Conservatives became convinced that provincial politics should be partisan politics. On 3 April 1903 Rutherford chaired the annual meeting of the Strathcona Liberal Association, and in the election of officers he was named honorary president.[54]

Early in 1904 the Strathcona Liberals held a convention to nominate a candidate to contest the new federal constituency of Strathcona in the forthcoming general election. Rutherford was offered but declined the nomination:

> Several of the gentlemen delegates expressed their regret that Mr. Rutherford had declined to accept nomination and it was very evident that from one end of the constituency to the other he was the first choice of the delegation.[55]

The convention finally nominated Peter Talbot of Lacombe, who, actively supported by Rutherford, went on to win the seat for the Liberals in the fall election. Provincial autonomy had been an important plank in the Liberal platform and three months after the election, in February 1905, Prime Minister Laurier introduced the Autonomy Bills that created the provinces of Alberta and Saskatchewan.

Rutherford's election to the territorial assembly had brought him increased public prominence; his activities were faithfully chronicled in the pages of the *Plaindealer*. In November 1902 he became a patron, together with Lord Strathcona, of the Strathcona Curling Club. In the spring of 1903 he was elected honorary president of the Strathcona Baseball Club, the Curling Club, and the Football Club. Photographs of his now substantial two-storey residence appeared in the 19 September 1902 and the 23 December 1904 issues of the *Plaindealer*. In June 1903, on his return from the legislative session in Regina, he was welcomed home with a banquet by the Strathcona Town Council.

Even after he became a member of the territorial Legislative Assembly, Rutherford continued to perform his duties as secretary-treasurer and solicitor for the Town of Strathcona. Because of the increased work load brought on by the growth of the town, his annual $600 salary was increased in January 1905 to $800. He easily earned it, being responsible for drafting numerous by-laws, such as By-law 121 that provided for the borrowing of $104,000 for town waterworks and sewers. It is noteworthy that early in 1902, when council was considering taking over the privately owned light system in Strathcona, Rutherford publicly urged the move on the grounds that it would result in lower utility rates and provide badly needed revenue for the town.[56] The theme of government involvement in utilities was to recur when Rutherford became premier of Alberta.

Figure 13: 360 Cooper Street, Ottawa, 1904
L-R Mattie, Hazel, Minnie Jarman (sister of Mrs. Rutherford), baby
Marjorie and Cecil
(Mrs. Hazel McCuaig)

The law partnership of Rutherford and Jamieson continued to prosper. In the spring of 1902 they were offering private and company loans. In July 1903 a law student named A. T. Mode articled with the firm,[57] and early in 1904 the offices were moved from the Parrish Block to the second floor of the Imperial Bank building at the corner of Whyte and Main.[58] When Miss Postle left the firm in 1902 because of ill health, Miss Fanny Martin replaced her as stenographer.

Beginning in 1902, Mrs. Rutherford was "at home"[59] for social occasions, and in April of that year the Rutherfords held an "entertainment" at their home for teachers and other friends. The party featured games that tested the participants' knowledge of literature and of the faces of literary and political leaders of the day. But the highlight of the evening was ping-pong, the latest English craze sweeping Canadian cities.[60] Two of Mrs. Rutherford's sisters were house guests in the summer of 1902, and the following year Rutherford's sister and a sister of Mrs. Rutherford's visited from Ontario. In June 1904 Mrs. Rutherford took her three children to Ottawa for three months: she had given birth to another daughter, Marjorie, in the fall of 1903 when she was approaching her thirty-eighth birthday.

Rutherford's abiding interest in education and books is demonstrated by his donation of a twenty-dollar book prize to the top graduating student in the Strathcona district in 1903, a gift he repeated the following year. He also donated awards to the Strathcona Curling Club and to the Strathcona Rifle Association. Rutherford was an ardent tennis player and also apparently a good curler: in March 1903 his rink won the Ochsner trophy. As a successful businessman in Strathcona, it is not surprising that he was elected to the council of the Strathcona Board of Trade in 1903. A devout Baptist all his life, he was able to find time to attend the two-day Alberta Baptist Association convention held in Wetaskiwin in September 1903. He was one of the more active members of the First Baptist Church of Strathcona, serving not only as deacon and trustee, but auditor as well. His duties included chairing the monthly business meetings of the church.

Thus the beginning of 1905 found Rutherford on the threshold of political power, yet still innocent of any political ambition. He had become an important and highly visible element in the social fabric of Strathcona: public spirited, capable, and always prepared to serve when called upon. Three years as a member of the Legislative Assembly had brought him into close contact with the major political figures in western Canada, and there can be no doubt that he favourably impressed his peers. Rutherford, in fact, stood with Frank Oliver and Peter Talbot as a major contender for the leadership of the as-yet unorganized Liberal party in the future province of Alberta.[62]

In January 1905 he went to Ottawa with fellow Strathcona lawyer D. H. McKinnon to enquire into Canadian Pacific, Canadian Northern, and Grand Trunk Pacific Railway plans in the Strathcona district. In answer to an urgent telegram Rutherford cut short his visit and returned to Strathcona. Two days after his return, his infant daughter Marjorie, scarcely sixteen months old, died of pneumonia.[63] McKinnon returned three weeks later, to report that in Ottawa it was assumed that party lines would be drawn in the first election in the new province and that Rutherford would likely be the Liberal leader in the first legislature.[64]

Subsequent events moved quickly. Laurier introduced the Autonomy Bills in February 1905. The clauses dealing with education immediately created dissension within Liberal ranks across the country. The act declared that separate territorial schools already existing in the territories would be perpetuated at public expense in the newly created provinces of Alberta and Saskatchewan. Conservative and Liberal critics alike saw in this a violation of provincial rights under the British North America Act, which set aside education as a provincial responsibility. Clifford Sifton, minister of the interior, resigned in protest, to be replaced on 8 April 1905 by Frank Oliver, M.P. for Edmonton. The education controversy was settled with an amendment that placed separate schools clearly under provincial control.

Far less palatable for westerners was the fact that the Autonomy Bills withheld lands and resources from the proposed new provinces. Laurier cited national policy and the purchase of the West by the Dominion as justification, but there were also compelling partisan motivations at work. The federal Conservatives and Haultain in the Territories had become champions of full provincial autonomy and Laurier could only give them a powerful advantage in forthcoming elections if he acceded to their demands.[65] The Liberal alternative proposed by Laurier took the form of generous federal grants in lieu of resources. Despite Conservative charges of coerciveness and second-class provincial status, the bills became the Alberta and Saskatchewan Acts and came into force on 1 September 1905. After having campaigned for full provincial autonomy, Rutherford could only have been dismayed by the result, but held his peace in the interest of party unity.

Now the stage had been set for Rutherford's central role in the making of the province of Alberta: as minister of the interior, Frank Oliver had fulfilled his political ambition; Peter Talbot, M.P. for Strathcona, had his eye on an appointment to the Senate (which he got in 1906); and both Oliver and Talbot supported Rutherford as the first leader of the party.[66] Rutherford was the man of the hour.

In August 1905 the Liberals in the proposed province met in Calgary for the founding convention of the Liberal Association of Alberta. The delegates, Rutherford included, were not impressed with Haultain's continued pleas for nonpartisan administrations in the new provinces. The territorial Conservatives had, after all, held a convention at Moose Jaw in March 1903 at which Haultain had been elected president, and in the 1904 federal election campaign Haultain had actively supported the Conservative cause. But more to the point, with the Liberals in power in Ottawa under Prime Minister Laurier it was a foregone conclusion that Liberal lieutenant-governors would be installed in both Alberta and Saskatchewan, and that they would call upon Liberal party leaders to form the first governments of those provinces. In short, the Liberal party delegates at Calgary knew that the man they elected president of the party would become the first premier of Alberta. They unanimously elected Alexander Cameron Rutherford, who characteristically accepted with the hope that he would not disappoint those who had chosen him.[67]

The unanimity at Calgary did not tell the whole story. Both Talbot and Oliver harboured private reservations about Rutherford's suitability as leader.[68] Laurier's advisors and George Bulyea, the lieutenant-governor designate, would have preferred Talbot as party leader.[69] Rutherford himself was terrified by the prospect of becoming premier, but allowed his name to stand for nomination from a sense of loyalty to his constituents. Indeed, the support he enjoyed in his constituency and his general popularity in northern Alberta was a matter of concern to Liberals in the south, who saw Rutherford as too much of an Edmonton man. And Alberta Liberals, especially their new leader, now faced the thankless prospect of having to defend the limited terms of autonomy granted by the federal government.

But partisanship was now the name of the game, and this was no time to be negative or divided. In an editorial published one week after the Liberal convention, the *Alberta Plaindealer* optimistically assessed the future premier:

> Strathcona is proud to number among her citizens one called to do so distinguished a duty as that of organizing the first government of the new Province. Mr. Rutherford is to be congratulated upon the honour that has

been bestowed upon him as a tribute to his integrity and qualifications as a public man. His modesty and retiring disposition are too well known to require comment and it is well known that from the beginning of his public career to the present time Mr. Rutherford has been pushed into positions of political prominence by his friends who recognize his qualifications. On the occasion of the Federal election he was the first choice of the Liberals from one end of the Strathcona constituency to the other but declined absolutely the honour when thrust upon him, an honour which went to Mr. Talbot. Again he is called by his fellows to come up higher, yes higher than before. His special qualifications for the office of the first minister make it absolutely necessary in the interests of the Province that he accept the responsibility now about to be conferred upon him. [70]

Rutherford, of course, would accept. He had really done so at Calgary a week before. Now forty-eight, with twenty years of legal practice behind him, he had become during a decade of public service one of the most respected figures in western Canada. His "special qualifications" for the office of premier, however, were to be found more in his personal qualities than in his proven political ability. Although he had been politically active for nearly a decade, he had served as an elected representative for a relatively short time, and his ability as a political leader had yet to be seriously tested. The next five years would provide that test.

CHAPTER II

ARCHITECT OF A PROVINCE (1905 - 1910)

At high noon on Friday, 1 September 1905, the province of Alberta came into being as Governor-General Earl Grey administered the oath of allegiance to the new lieutenant-governor, George H. V. Bulyea, at the exhibition grounds in Edmonton. A twenty-one gun salute immediately signalled that the Districts of Alberta and Athabasca together had been officially elevated from territorial to provincial status. Speeches by Earl Grey, Prime Minister Laurier, Bulyea, and others proclaimed the historic importance of the occasion. Residents of the new province celebrated by playing baseball, lacrosse, and polo, and by applauding the equestrian prowess of the Royal North-West Mounted Police in their musical ride.[1]

These ceremonies and celebrations had been preceded by weeks of feverish planning and preparation. Two weeks after the Liberals held their convention at Calgary, the Conservatives met at Red Deer, agreed on a platform, and named their leader. He was Richard Bedford Bennett, a Calgary lawyer, solicitor for the C.P.R. and the Bell Telephone Company, and future prime minister. Then the federal government announced the appointment of Bulyea as lieutenant-governor designate for Alberta. A former territorial M.L.A. and a staunch Liberal, Bulyea could be depended on to call another Liberal to form the first provincial government. Throughout the province, party conventions were held to select candidates to contest the twenty-five constituencies in the forthcoming provincial election. Most candidates were Ontarians. On 29 August the Strathcona Liberals met and declared A. C. Rutherford their candidate by acclamation.[2] Rutherford, always the reluctant politician, thanked the convention for their confidence in him and typically expressed his hope that they might not have cause to regret it.

Figure 14: First Lieutenant-Governor and Executive Council of Alberta, 1905. (Provincial Archives of Alberta, A.1382)

Minister of Agriculture and
Provincial Secretary
William T. Finlay

Attorney-General
Charles W. Cross

Premier
Alexander C. Rutherford

Lieutenant-Governor
George H. V. Bulyea

Minister of Public Works
William H. Cushing

Minister without Portfolio
Leverett G. DeVeber

Rutherford had been even busier than usual. In Calgary on 23 August he had attended the founding meeting of the Provincial Lord's Day Alliance, and had been elected one of its vice-presidents, along with R. B. Bennett.[3] From there he had toured the southern parts of the new province and then went on to Regina, where he recruited staff for the new provincial departments from among officials of the now moribund territorial administration.[4] Then too, as a member of the Inaugural Ceremony Committee, he was directly involved in planning the 1 September proceedings at the exhibition grounds.

On the morning of Saturday, 2 September, Lieutenant-Governor Bulyea made it his first official act to call on A. C. Rutherford to form a provincial government. Rutherford accepted and was immediately sworn in as premier of Alberta. That same evening the citizens of Strathcona organized a demonstration on behalf of their first citizen. A torchlight procession headed by the fire brigade band marched to Rutherford's house, serenaded him, and then accompanied him to a nearby bonfire, where he was cheered and eulogized to the sounds of exploding rockets and band music.[5]

On 6 September Rutherford announced his cabinet. It included a lawyer, Charles W. Cross, as attorney-general; two businessmen, William H. Cushing (minister of public works) and William T. Finlay (minister of agriculture and provincial secretary); and Dr. George DeVeber as minister without portfolio. Premier Rutherford retained the portfolios of treasury and education for himself. Southern Alberta was well represented in his cabinet: Calgary by Cushing, Medicine Hat by Finlay, and Lethbridge by DeVeber. Cross represented Edmonton. Despite the sizeable ethnic elements within the population, the ministers were all English-speaking Protestants. Two of the ministers, Cross and Cushing, were political novices[6] and, like Rutherford, natives of Ontario.

The Alberta Act had named Edmonton provisional capital of the province, and already a train carload of books and documents from the dismantled territorial government had arrived in the city. Several former territorial officials had also arrived from Regina to take up their duties in the provincial capital.[7] But before the mountain of necessary founding legislation could be passed, there was a provincial election to be held. It was called for 9 November 1905. The Liberals, as creatures of the federal government that had defined the terms of autonomy, went into the campaign as defenders of the Alberta Act against Conservative criticism. Not only had the act imposed separate schools in Alberta, it withheld control of lands, mines, and minerals from the new province, for which Alberta was to be compensated $375,000 annually. The financial terms also included annual grants for governmental expenses and public buildings, and a grant in lieu of debt liquidation (Alberta was born debt-free), making a total annual claim on the federal government of more than a million dollars.[8]

The Conservatives attacked both the invasion of provincial rights inherent in the imposed separate schools, and the second-class status of a province without control of its resources. The Liberals, notably Premier Rutherford, argued that education and separate schools were clearly under provincial control, and that the generous financial terms of autonomy made Alberta financially secure even without control of its resources. Compelled by partisan considerations to take this stand, Rutherford undoubtedly held private reservations, but he was willing to try this federal approach. Meanwhile, Conservative Leader R. B. Bennett was even more vulnerable because of his connections with the C. P. R. and other unpopular corporations. The Liberals easily manipulated the issues in the election by alleging that the hated, tax-exempt C.P.R. was the real force behind the Conservatives. The Liberals held another valuable advantage: as custodians of the provincial government, they were able to wield the sword of political patronage, an asset denied the Conservatives.[9] With so many positions to be filled in the administration of the infant province, there was a powerful incentive to work for the Liberal cause.

The election results surprised even the optimistic Liberals. They won twenty-three of the twenty-five seats, the Conservatives winning only two. Conservative Leader Bennett was defeated in Calgary by Public Works Minister Cushing. Premier Rutherford had been given a clear mandate and a virtually opposition-free Legislative Assembly with which to govern the province for the next four years. Once again the town of Strathcona honoured its favourite son. Escorted by a torch-lit procession, the premier, his wife, and his daughter Hazel were taken by carriage to a bonfire, where once more the night echoed with the name "Rutherford."[10] The voters of Alberta had unknowingly elected only the first of many huge majorities to their provincial assembly, and for now at least the Liberals were the beneficiaries.

The time had come for Rutherford to relinquish his position as Strathcona's secretary-treasurer. In early January 1906 he attended his last council meeting, swore in the recently elected mayor and councillors, and said farewell. He was replaced as secretary-treasurer by George F. Downes, but Downes declined the solicitorship that Rutherford had carried so well for six years. During the latter's tenure there had not been a single lawsuit involving the town, a tribute to his legal skill and conciliatory attitude.[11]

The opening session of the first legislature of Alberta (1906 - 1909) convened at 3:00 p.m. on 15 March 1906 at the Thistle Rink in Edmonton, where over four thousand people heard Lieutenant-Governor Bulyea read the speech from the throne.[12] After an hour's sitting, the house adjourned until the following day. Premier and Mrs. Rutherford, together with cabinet ministers and their wives, then held a reception in the assembly hall on the third floor of the new McKay Avenue School.[13] The 16 March issue of the *Strathcona Plaindealer* described the reception as

a brilliant affair and an unqualified success. Upwards of a thousand ladies and gentlemen attended and were received by the Premier and his cabinet. Clarke's orchestra was present and made melody for the occasion. Light refreshments were served, many of the young ladies and gentlemen of the Government clerical staff being the waiters in attendance.

Figure 15: Opening of the First Legislature of Alberta, Thistle Rink,
            15 March 1906.
            (Provincial Archives of Alberta, H74-29-2)

LT. GOV. BULYEA AND MEMBERS
OF ALBERTA'S FIRST LEGISLATIVE ASSEMBLY
(PLUS A COUPLE OF EDMONTON MAYORS)

ERNEST BROWN
PHOTO EDMONTON
B-10550

Figure 16: Lieutenant-Governor Bulyea and members of the First Legislative Assembly of Alberta, McKay Avenue School, 9 May 1906. (Provincial Archives of Alberta, B.6663)

The McKay Avenue School was to serve as Alberta's temporary legislature until 1908, when the newly completed Terrace Building was ready to accommodate the third session.[14] Alberta's permanent legislative chamber was first used in December 1911 but the entire legislative building was not completed until 1913. Ironically, though he had considerable influence on the location and design of the legislative building,[15] Rutherford would never sit as premier in its ornate chamber.

While the Alberta Act had named Edmonton provisional capital of the province, it fell to the Legislative Assembly to make a permanent selection. Calgary and Edmonton were the chief contenders, but Red Deer and Banff had their supporters too. In its first session in April 1906, the legislature made the fateful decision when the Honourable William Cushing's motion that the capital be permanently located at Calgary was defeated sixteen to eight; motions for Red Deer and Banff were withdrawn when they failed to find enough support.[16] Edmonton had prevailed, but the decision rankled in Calgary.

The primary task facing the apprentice legislature was to establish the statutory and administrative foundations of the new province, a tedious and demanding procedure that kept the assembly busy until 9 May. Rutherford, with the advantages of his experience in the territorial assembly, his legal training and familiarity with the statutes of the older provinces, and his large majority, easily guided the detailed bills through the house. The token opposition could scarcely oppose this founding legislation in any case, for it was all essential and based on strong precedent. The first session and those that followed were stamped with the virtues personified by the premier: serious dedication, respect for tradition, and a dogged determination to get things done.

Rutherford played a central role in the first legislature. As first minister, provincial treasurer, and minister of education, he was charged with heavy responsibilities. In addition, he served on most of the standing committees of the house. Indeed, in the second session (1907), he was a member of all nine standing committees: privileges and elections, railways, miscellaneous and private bills, agriculture and colonization, standing orders, public accounts, printing, municipal law, and local bills. During the course of the four sessions of the first legislature, he personally introduced no less than forty bills, including those to establish the treasury department, the public service, the university, and public libraries.

As provincial treasurer Rutherford presented the budget in each session of the first legislature, performing the task with considerable authority and skill, thanks in no small part to his years as secretary-treasurer for the Town of Strathcona. In the first years of provincehood, provincial expenditures totalled from $2 million to $2.8 million annually, about half of which came from Ottawa in grants according to the terms of autonomy.[17] While Rutherford consistently defended those terms, including the grant in lieu of lands, he also looked for new sources of provincial revenue, notably in the form of corporation taxes. His aim was to keep Alberta debt-free by presenting a balanced budget with a comfortable surplus in case of contingencies. His eventual departure from this principle, in the form of government involvement in telephones

Premier Rutherford : " Pay no heed, gentlemen, to those irresponsible papers which say that—

The Alberta Government is about to have —

A FALL ! ! ! ! ! !

Figure 17: The Morang School-book contract viewed by the *Calgary Eye Opener*, 18 July 1908.
(Glenbow-Alberta Institute)

Figure 18: The school-book issue seen by the *Calgary Eye Opener,* 5 September 1908.
(Glenbow-Alberta-Institute)

and railways, saddled future governments with debts and deficits.[18] Rutherford's fiscal philosophy could be generally characterized as cautious and conservative, but it was marked with examples of calculated risk-taking that in time proved riskier than he had expected.

As he had long advocated, Rutherford introduced legislation in 1906 to tax railways within the province, including the C.P.R. He anticipated a revenue of $160,000. The C.P.R. fought the legislation through its solicitor, R. B. Bennett, all the way to the Privy Council. In 1911 the Council ruled that the tax was beyond the powers of the province to levy.[19] A more reliable source of revenue for Rutherford was the income from government-owned creameries, which ran close to $250,000 annually.[20]

Education claimed from 10 to 14 per cent of government expenditures. As minister of education, Rutherford was committed to seeing that school facilities kept pace with the province's rapidly growing population, and this commitment was reflected in the phenomenal growth of the school system during his tenure. On 1 September 1905 there were 526 schools in Alberta; three years later there were more than 1,000.[21] A major thrust of this expansion was the provision of schools for the burgeoning Ukrainian population, chiefly in the districts northeast of Edmonton. During a five-month period in 1906, 16 schools were established in predominantly Ukrainian-speaking areas of the province. Much of this development was due to the work of Robert Fletcher, engaged by Rutherford in 1906 as supervisor of schools among the Ukrainian immigrants of the province.[22] Convinced that education was the basis of intelligent citizenship and the foundation of good government, Rutherford took these initiatives to facilitate the integration of the large Ukrainian population into Alberta society.

Following a conference of the education ministers of the three prairie provinces in November 1907, Rutherford took the first step towards the introduction of free, uniform school texts in the West. He decided to purchase new readers "more in harmony with the condition of things in the West" than were the old Ontario readers then in use.[23] Rutherford was criticized for not having the readers published in Alberta (the contract went to the Morang Company in Toronto), but he defended the action on the grounds of cost and quality, and offered to subsidize any Alberta firm that could even approximate the standards demanded in the contract.

Of all his efforts in the field of education, however, Rutherford's "darling project" was the establishment of the provincial university. He personally introduced the university bill in the first session of the legislature in 1906, and guided it through to royal assent in spite of widespread opposition, even in the Liberal columns of the *Edmonton Bulletin*. As Rutherford later recalled:

> On every hand there was a strong feeling there was no necessity for such an institution at that time: that the idea had been launched too soon. My reason for insistence on immediate action was that I had in mind the bickerings which had occurred in Ontario and Manitoba when their universities were projected

and wished to avoid the mistake of having various religious sects erect their own colleges. This we succeeded in doing by reason of quick decision. In a few years the majority of those who had been in opposition to the plan of an early start for the institution had changed their minds and approved the policy behind its erection.[24]

Thus the new university was to be non-denominational and co-educational.

Its founding act, however, did not specify where the university would be located. Rutherford's request for a land endowment from the federal government was refused by Laurier with the comment that, thanks to federal subsidies, "the provinces of Alberta and Saskatchewan are now more wealthy than the Dominion Government."[25] It was not until 6 April 1907, three weeks after the second session of the legislature had been prorogued, that Rutherford announced that Strathcona, only recently incorporated as a city, would be the site of the university. He had in fact been negotiating for the 258-acre Simpson estate two kilometres west of his office for some months, but he knew that the choice would antagonize Calgary Liberals, particularly his minister of public works, the Honourable William Cushing.

Calgarians were indeed enraged by the announcement, for this was the second rebuff they had suffered at the hands of the Rutherford administration. First they had lost the battle for the provincial capital, and now, a year later, they saw their hopes for the university dashed. The fact that Calgary had been chosen as the site for the new $85,000 Normal School was little consolation. Politically, Rutherford's decisions to have a university and to locate it in Strathcona were to cost him dearly, yet that institution remained his source of greatest personal satisfaction and pride.[26]

It was in the telephone system that Rutherford's administration showed its first real departure from tradition and the safe course. When Alberta became a province there were already a number of small private or municipal telephone systems in operation, notably the Bell Telephone Company, centred at Calgary. Rural and long-distance lines were virtually nonexistent. In the first speech from the throne, the government announced its intention to make telephonic communication as widespread and effective as possible. To this end the assembly passed a Telephone Act that allocated $25,000 for preliminary work on a government-owned service in long-distance lines, and empowered municipalities to establish and operate their own telephone systems.[27] By 1908 the government had not only constructed almost 2,250 kilometres of long-distance lines and more than 1,125 kilometres of rural party lines, but had also purchased three exchanges and bought the entire Bell system for $675,000.[28]

While the first government-owned telephone system in Canada was a going concern, it nevertheless could not be financed out of general revenue. Late in 1908 the government issued debentures for $2 million at 4 per cent over thirty years, thus abandoning its pay-as-you-go policy.[29] Although Rutherford himself was obviously committed to the venture, Public Works Minister Cushing was its prime mover and most vociferous advocate, for it was his department that built and operated the system.

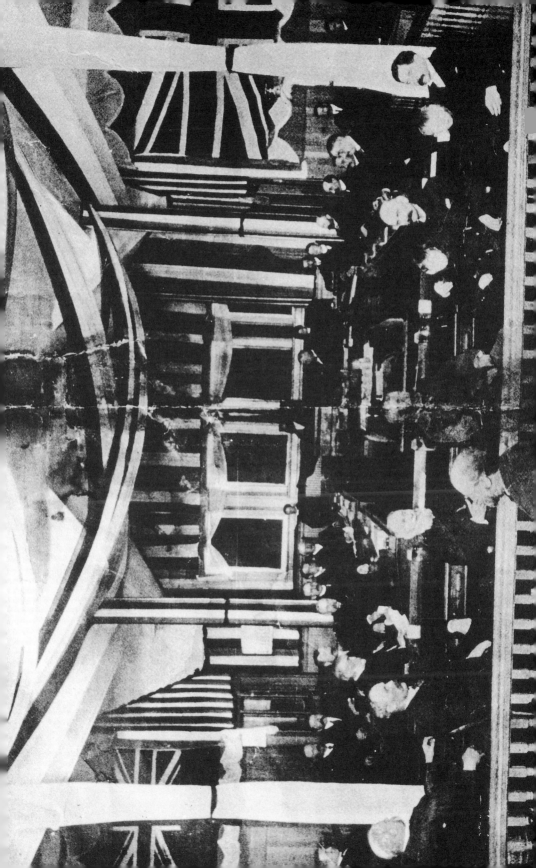

Figure 19: Second Session of the First Legislature of Alberta, McKay Avenue
School, 1907.
(*Edmonton Daily Bulletin,* Christmas 1907)

Indeed, by 1908 Rutherford was cautioned by Senator Peter Talbot that Cushing was "going crazy" on government ownership and that money on telephones would have been better spent on roads and ditches. Talbot's remark, "If you don't keep a check on him you will some day find a lot of trouble through him," would prove prophetic.[30]

As a result of the primitive stage of the infrastructure and the rapid growth of population in Alberta during the first years of provincial status, the Department of Public Works predictably accounted for a large share of government spending. Roads, bridges, public buildings, and other facilities regularly ate up more than 40 per cent of Rutherford's expenditures, but this was consistent with the policy of improved communications he had advocated as early at 1896, when he first sought election to the territorial assembly.

Alberta's predominantly rural population was the object of much of the legislation passed by the Rutherford administration; indeed, the heavy representation of farmer M.L.A.s guaranteed sympathy for farm interests in the legislature. Rutherford himself introduced a bill in the first session authorizing the use of $250,000 as a bonus or subsidy for sugar beet producers in southern Alberta. A similar amount was authorized for the expansion of government creameries in the same session. The legislature approved grants for farmers' exhibitions and fairs, a grant of $20,000 to aid agricultural societies, and a proposed expenditure of $50,000 for a pork packing plant. [31]

By contrast, the Rutherford government's labour legislation was less progressive. Strikes in the coal mining industry in 1906 and 1907 resulted in a fuel shortage, and prompted the government to appoint a commission to look into conditions in the mines. Although reform legislation was passed in 1908 limiting the work day in the mines to eight hours, many other conditions affecting the mine workers were ignored. A Workmen's Compensation Act passed in the same session placed severe limitations on the amount of compensation payable and the conditions of eligibility. As L. G. Thomas concluded: "The legislature showed little sympathy with labour and little interest in labour problems, except when these made the general public uncomfortable."[32]

The first automobiles made their appearance on Edmonton streets in 1904. Subsequently, during the first legislative session, the Rutherford government passed a bill to regulate the speed and operation of motor vehicles. The maximum highway speed was set at twenty miles (thirty-two kilometres) per hour; within the corporate limits of towns and cities, it was reduced to ten miles (sixteen kilometres) per hour. All vehicles were to be equipped with proper alarm bells, gongs, or horns. Though Rutherford himself never learned to drive, he was an early automobile owner and his large red Packard was a familiar sight on Edmonton streets for many years. Cecil and Hazel were his frequent chauffeurs.[33]

By 1908 the need for railways had become the most urgent preoccupation in Alberta for government and people alike. Agricultural, industrial, and community growth had far outstripped the limited railway facilities of the province: if growth were to continue and Alberta were to realize its golden destiny, something had to be done

Figure 20: Dr. Rutherford's red Packard, c. 1912.
            Cecil at the wheel, Hazel at the extreme left, and four members of the
            Martin family.
            (Mrs. Helen Rutherford)

Figure 21: Lieutenant-Governor Bulyea, Lord Strathcona and Premier Ruther-
            ford at Government House, 7 September, 1909.
            (PAA B.8635)

to encourage the construction of new lines. The Rutherford government had been pondering the issue since 1905. During the 1907 session it had passed a Railway Act that authorized the Minister of Public Works to permit the construction of railways anywhere in the province by any company whose plans he approved. But the act had produced no new lines.[34] The Conservative opposition advocated government ownership and operation of railways, but the Liberals looked to Ottawa for a solution: could not the federal government encourage railway construction by providing loans, grants, or guarantees? By November 1908 it was clear that Ottawa was not prepared to do so, and Rutherford made this announcement:

> I have given the railway question a great deal of thought during the past year, and have thoroughly weighed the advantages of immediate railway construction. I have now decided upon a policy of railway extension throughout all parts of the Province, and you are at liberty to say that I will give my best endeavours to the advancement of this project. I intend to establish a Department of Railways, and to make it one of the most important departments of the government, and one which I will personally look after. It is very plain that the next stage of progress in this Province and the development of its real possibilities will depend mainly upon railway extension.

> In the past three years we have undertaken various necessary projects, but now the great need of the Province is railways. Men will not build railways in a new country, however, without some government assistance. They will demand that their bonds be guaranteed, and the only source[s] to which they can look for this help in Albertan lines are the Federal Government and our own. We have been for some time asking the Federal Government to extend this assistance, and we will continue to do so. But if Ottawa will not help us, then we will do it ourselves. The railways must be built.[35]

Three months later, in the dying moments of the first legislature, Rutherford unveiled his government's eagerly awaited railway policy. The government would guarantee the bonds of three railway companies chartered to build lines in Alberta: the Grand Trunk Pacific (G.T.P.), the Canadian Northern (C.N.), and the Alberta and Great Waterways Railway (A. & G.W.). The G.T.P. and the C.N. guarantees were to be at $13,000 a mile for a total of 1,411 miles (2,271 kilometres). Interest on the bonds would be 4 per cent for a term of thirty years. With legislative approval, the guarantee could be increased to $15,000 a mile. The A. & G.W. guarantee would be at $20,000 a mile for 350 miles (563 kilometres), with interest at 5 per cent for a term of fifty years. An additional $400,000 would be guaranteed for the construction of a terminal in Edmonton. To earn this money, the companies had to meet specified deadlines: G.T.P. and C.N. lines were to be completed by the end of 1911, A. & G.W. by 1913. Proceeds from the sale of the bonds were to be placed in banks to the credit of the provincial treasurer, and would be paid to the companies as construction proceeded. And the province would be secured with a first mortgage on rolling stock, terminals, and other assets.[36] This policy, and the legislative acts that implemented it, were acclaimed as a safe, economical means of promoting railway development in the province.

On this crest of public optimism the first legislature was dissolved and elections were called for 22 March 1909. Rutherford and the Liberals went to the people on their record of safe, honest government and the new era of prosperity to be ushered in by the railway policy: "Rutherford, Reliability and Railways."[37]

Rutherford's appeal to the "gentlemen" electors (women remained unenfranchised until 1916 in Alberta) was characteristic:

> It is now three and a half years since you accepted my promise to do all that in me lay for the welfare of the Province of Alberta. I appeal to your justice whether I have or have not fulfilled that promise. If you now renew your acceptance of myself and my colleagues as the custodians of your public affairs, you may rest assured that those affairs will be my sole consideration and care in a further term of office.[38]

Rutherford spent a good part of the campaign in such southern Conservative strongholds as Calgary, Lethbridge, and Pincher Creek, speaking on behalf of his colleagues. His nomination on 13 March at Strathcona was a mere formality, attended by as many enthusiastic Conservatives and independents as Liberals from all over the constituency.[39] The Conservatives throughout the province were in serious disarray and were unable even to draft a party leader for the campaign; R. B. Bennett was unable to spare the time, but he did stand for election in Calgary.[40] On the eve of the election, Rutherford's final appeal to the electorate was published in the *Strathcona Plaindealer*:

> I appeal to you for the elimination of selfish and partisan considerations. I appeal to you not as Liberals or Conservatives, but as Albertans. The Province must stand before the party.[41]

For ardently partisan Liberals, especially federal Liberals who faced a contest soon against a revitalized Conservative party, such sentiments expressed by a provincial party leader were dangerous and irresponsible. Not only was Rutherford undermining the primacy of the two-party system, he was raising the spectre of western nationalism in its place.

On that troubling note the Liberals were swept back into power. In a Legislative Assembly expanded to forty-one seats by redistribution, thirty-seven Liberals and two Conservatives (including R. B. Bennett) were elected, with the remaining two seats going to Edward Michener, an Independent Conservative from Red Deer, and C. M. O'Brien, a Socialist from the mining constituency of Rocky Mountain.[42] Rutherford himself received 85 per cent of the ballots cast in Strathcona. As the *Plaindealer* put it: "Rutherford is supreme."[43]

Figure 22: Imperial Conference on Education convened by the League of the Empire, London , 1907. (University of Alberta Archives, 73-165)

But Rutherford was also suspect, and his supremacy was to endure but a year longer, until the spring of 1910. His fall, stunning in its unexpectedness, would end nearly five years of intense political activity and public prominence. As premier of Alberta from 1905 to 1910, he was not only the dominant figure in the provincial legislature and the Liberal party, but the principal representative and spokesman of a rapidly growing province. For Rutherford they were five years of unprecedented responsibility and opportunity. Scarcely a year after becoming premier he had attended a conference of provincial premiers in Ottawa to discuss federal grants to the provinces. Rutherford and his eight colleagues evidently made a good case for the provinces, for out of the conference came substantial increases in the subsidies, Alberta's share being $130,000 annually.[44] In May 1907 he attended an education conference in London, England, organized by the League of the Empire, where he conferred with educational leaders from Britain and many parts of the empire.[45] Rutherford, accompanied by his family, used the occasion to visit his ancestral home at Aberfeldy, Scotland, and to tour the continent.[46] In November of the same year Rutherford attended a conference of prairie education ministers and school-book publishers in Winnipeg, which resulted in the introduction of a new common reader in Alberta and Saskatchewan the following year. From Winnipeg Rutherford went on to Columbus, Ohio, where he attended a convention of the International Tax Association. The members elected him vice-president of the organization.[47] On this occasion he visited Ohio State University at Columbus in search of ideas for the proposed provincial university. En route home he also inspected the capital buildings in St. Paul, Minnesota, examined by Public Works Minister Cushing the year before, that inspired the design of Alberta's legislative building.[48]

Organized pressure from prairie grain growers to have the privately owned and operated grain elevators purchased and expanded by the provincial governments necessitated two prairie premiers' conferences in 1908. The premiers jointly refused the proposal on the grounds that it might not be constitutional, and that raising the required capital would consequently prove impossible.[49] In July 1908 Rutherford formally opened the Winnipeg fair. Then, as Alberta's official representatives, he and Lieutenant-Governor Bulyea attended the Quebec City tercentenary celebrations, in which the Prince of Wales also participated.[50] Again in 1909 Rutherford and Bulyea were Alberta's official representatives at the International Irrigation Conference held in August in Spokane.[51]

In September 1907 the University of Toronto conferred on Rutherford the honorary degree of Doctor of Laws in recognition of his contributions to the field of higher education in Alberta. On his arrival home from Toronto, the now "Honourable Doctor" found a letter from McMaster University informing him that the same honorary degree was about to be granted to him by that institution. Unfortunately he was unable to return east to receive the honour.[52] A year later a third LL.D. degree was conferred on him, this time by the fledgling University of Alberta, temporarily based at the Duggan Street School in Strathcona.[53] Much later in his life, in October 1931,

Rutherford received yet another honorary LL.D., from McGill University whence he had graduated exactly half a century before.

Having guided the university bill through the legislature in 1906, and arranged in 1907 for the province to purchase the $150,000 Simpson estate as a university site, Rutherford now found in Dr. Henry Marshall Tory the ideal person to carry his dream to realization. Tory, like Rutherford, was a graduate of McGill, and was now a professor of physics and mathematics at that university. Rutherford had first met Tory in 1905 and had been impressed with his views on the need for non-denominational state-endowed universities in the new provinces. Dr. Tory was appointed president of the proposed university in 1907 by order in council. Members of the first convocation were graduates of British and Canadian universities resident in Alberta. This assembly, 364 in number, elected a chancellor and 5 members of the university senate, while the government appointed 10 others. Rutherford and Tory were ex officio members of the senate.[54] Its first meeting, in March 1908, was chaired by Chancellor C. A. Stuart, a justice of the Alberta Supreme Court. The senate decided that classes in the first- and second-year Arts and Sciences should commence in the fall of 1908. Rutherford announced that he would give a one-hundred-dollar scholarship to the student with the highest standing in the matriculation examinations, the award to be known as the Rutherford Scholarship.[55] By September 1908 Tory had hired a faculty of four, purchased some necessary equipment, found temporary accommodation in the new Duggan Street (Queen Alexandra) School, and registered some two dozen students, with immediate prospects for another twenty. Included among the freshmen of 1908 was Cecil Rutherford. At the opening of the university, Premier Rutherford announced that he would donate a collection of books by Canadian authors to the university library, a gift that President Tory said would cost $5,000 to complete.[56] Rutherford's abiding personal interest in the development of the university library is also reflected in his surviving correspondence (1909, 1910) with Lord Strathcona, the Library of Parliament in Ottawa, and various legislative libraries. Through these contacts, he was able to acquire valuable governmental publications for the library.[57]

In January 1909 the university was moved to more spacious accommodation on the second floor of the new Strathcona Collegiate; Rutherford had laid the cornerstone of this school in October 1907.[58] On 29 September 1909 the Premier turned the sod for the university Arts Building, and work began immediately. By January 1910 the foundation was completed,[59] but developments in the legislature intervened and the Arts Building eventually became a casualty in Rutherford's fall from power. By 1913 a new design for the Arts Building had been prepared and the original foundation was demolished. Meanwhile, work had begun in 1910 on a student residence (Athabasca Hall) nearby, and when completed in 1912 it became the first permanent university building on the campus.

Ceremonies marking the commencement or completion of various public facilities were frequent during the early years of provincehood, and Rutherford often presided at them. For example, in August 1907 he laid the cornerstone for a new school in

Figure 23: First Convocation of the University of Alberta, 1908.
Front row, left to right: J.H. Riddell, H.M. Tory, A.L. Sifton, N.D.D.
Beck, C.A. Stuart, G.H.V. Bulyea, A.C. Rutherford.
(Mrs. Hazel McCuaig)

Figure 24: First Senate of the University of Alberta, 1908. Front row, left to
right: J.H. Riddell, A.C. Rutherford, H.M. Tory, C.A. Stuart, N.D.D.
Beck, J.A. McDougall.
(University of Alberta Archives, 69-12-225)

Figure 25: Queen Alexandra Elementery School, original home of the University of Alberta, September–December 1908.
(Historic Sites Service, 79R267-16)

Figure 26: Old Scona Academic High School, formerly Strathcona Collegiate, second location of the University of Alberta, 1909–1912.
(Glenbow-Alberta Institute, NA-1328-722)

Lacombe. He officially opened the bridge over the South Saskatchewan River at Medicine Hat in May 1908, and he opened another school in Lethbridge in April 1909. Edmonton author Eugenie Myles recounts the story of another ceremony that was first told by Bob Edwards in the *Eye Opener* of Calgary:

> Premier Rutherford and W. H. Cushing of Calgary, his minister of public works, on a certain day in 1906 journeyed by rig some 100 miles [160 kilometres] from Edmonton to Morningside near Red Deer, to open up a new much needed steel bridge. This "dinky culvert," as Edwards dubbed the bridge, was so small that the party of legislators drove right over it without recognizing it and had to double back for the ceremonial.

> Mirthfully, he went on to report that Cushing, with tears in his eyes, turned to Rutherford saying, "Alexander, you may go down to posterity as the founder of a great university, but the name of Cushing will live in honoured and imperishable memory as the father of the Morningside culvert."[60]

On 1 October 1909, two days after turning the sod for the ill-fated Arts Building, Rutherford played a prominent part in the ceremonies attending the laying of the cornerstone for Alberta's permanent legislative building. Three years earlier he had successfully negotiated the purchase from the Hudson's Bay Company of a twenty-one-acre (nine hectare) site overlooking Fort Edmonton, at a price of $4,000 an acre.[61] He had been intimately involved in the subsequent development of a design for the legislature, a design that was first made public in December 1907.[62] With evident satisfaction, he witnessed the laying of the cornerstone by Governor-General Earl Grey, to whom Rutherford then presented an address on behalf of the government of Alberta.[63] Three days later he was in Regina to participate in the equivalent ceremony for the Saskatchewan legislature.

In spite of the manifest demands on his time, Premier Rutherford continued to be an active Christian servant. In November 1907 he and Mrs. Rutherford attended the Western Baptist Convention in Calgary. A year later he chaired a meeting at the Strathcona Baptist Church to discuss the laymen's missionary movement, and in Vancouver a few days later he attended the Baptist Convention for western Canada, at which he was elected president of the convention.[64] Only a year previously he had been elected a vice-president of the Dominion Lord's Day Alliance at the annual meeting in Toronto.[65] Throughout his term as premier of Alberta, Rutherford served as a deacon in the First Baptist Church of Strathcona.

Meanwhile, the firm of Rutherford and Jamieson continued to provide legal services, though it is unlikely that Rutherford himself was an active partner during the period 1905–1910. In 1906 A. T. Mode, who had begun articling with the firm in the summer of 1903, was admitted to the Alberta bar; he became a partner in September of that year.[66] A month later another student, C. H. Grant, began articling with the

Figure 27: Turning the sod for the Arts Building, University of Alberta, 29 September 1909. (University of Alberta Archives, 69-12-224)

Figure 28: First student body, University of Alberta, 1908.
            Cecil Rutherford at extreme right.
            (Mrs. Helen Rutherford)

Figure 29: Premier Rutherford laying the cornerstone of the new public school,
            Lacombe, 21 August 1907.
            (Glenbow-Alberta Institute, ND-2-37)

firm.[67] In September 1908 Strathcona got its first automatic (dial) telephones and the Rutherford firm had one installed.[68]

Mrs. Rutherford shared in her husband's social prominence. Her receptions and teas were highlights of the social season and those who attended represented the most prestigious and respected members of Strathcona and Edmonton society. On Wednesday, 27 January 1909, for example,

> Mrs. Rutherford was "At Home" to a large number of Strathcona and Edmonton friends. The hostess received her guests in the drawing room in her own delightful way. She wore a beautiful gown of cream silk crepe de chene with trimmings of Irish point lace and cream satin ribbon. Mrs. Tory, who received with her, wore a handsome pink silk gown with trimmings of rich embroidery and green velvet ribbon. In the tea room, Mrs. Broadus and Mrs. J. M. Douglas poured tea and coffee. The former wore a cream gown....

The lengthy guest list included such prominent names as Bulyea, Hardisty, Sifton, and Cross.[69] A year later Mrs. Rutherford was elected honorary vice-president of the newly formed Women's Educational Association. The organization was composed of women with college degrees who wished to promote education in the province.[70] Later, this group became the Alberta Women's Association, and then the University Women's Club.[71]

Both Rutherford children were sent to Baptist colleges in Ontario. Cecil Rutherford attended Woodstock College for three years and graduated in May 1908, thirty years after his father.[72] He then enrolled at the University of Alberta in its first year of operation, not because he wanted to, but because his father insisted; his own preference was McGill.[73] In September 1908, accompanied by her father, fifteen-year-old Hazel Rutherford went to Toronto where she remained to attend Moulton Ladies' College for one year.[74]

As a businessman, Rutherford made a number of profitable real estate transactions in 1907. In February of that year he sold two commercial lots in Strathcona for a total of $30,000, and a quarter section just east of town for $22,000.[75] Speaking of these sales later at a Strathcona Board of Trade banquet given in his honour, Rutherford reassured his audience that he had not lost faith in Strathcona. On the contrary, he was still buying property in the city, but some of his early property investments were keeping him poor and he had merely decided "to relieve the grind" by selling them.[76] A few days later he offered the city a gift of five to ten acres from his farm adjoining Mill Creek, to be used as a park.[77] Renovations to the Rutherford Block on the southwest corner of Whyte Avenue and Main Street were started in the spring of 1907, including the addition of a concrete foundation that raised the building three feet. That summer the Dominion Bank occupied the front premises.[78]

After having visited Banff a number of times, Rutherford hired J. Luckett in the spring of 1908 to build a summer cottage in the park village. The two-storey frame

Figure 30: Mattie Rutherford, c. 1910.
(Mrs. Hazel McCuaig)

cottage was completed in time for the family and their guests to enjoy that summer,[79] and for many summers after. For Rutherford the cottage represented a haven far from the constant pressures of government business. In typical Rutherford style, he generously made it available to the faculty of the university. The cottage still stands at 525 Buffalo Street in Banff, overlooking the Bow River.

In 1909, at the peak of his political career, Rutherford decided to have a new house built. In May of that year he acquired a 1.3-acre (0.5-hectare) triangular plot from the farm of Laurent Garneau, which adjoined the university grounds and overlooked the site of the future legislative building. He had apparently planned to build on his property in what is now Bonnie Doon, but finally decided in favour of the university site, partly because it was more accessible at that time.[80] He hired Wilson and Herrald, a firm of British architects who had established an office on Whyte Avenue two years earlier,[81] to design the house, and by October 1909 they had completed the architectural plans for a two-storey mansion. Later that month the spectacle of the excavation for a premier's residence and the nearby foundation of a university attracted throngs of Sunday sightseers from both sides of the river.

"I do not see how the outlook...could be more promising," Rutherford had written at the end of 1906, concluding, "There is not as far as one can see a single cloud on the horizon."[82] At the close of 1909 both his and Alberta's prospects seemed equally bright. Rutherford could contemplate the developments of the past four years with justified satisfaction. Premier, treasurer, education minister, and now minister of railways, more than anyone he had guided Alberta through its transition from district to province. His personal contributions in the field of founding legislation were inestimable. The school system, university, legislature, and telephone system represented only a few of his personal triumphs. He had twice led his party to stunning election victories. As the province's chief spokesman and representative, he had received warm recognition in Canada and abroad. He had acquired new offices and honours, and his personal popularity among Albertans had soared. And now, to crown these achievements, his new railway policy held out the promise of unprecedented prosperity for the young province.

Figure 31: Cecil Rutherford at
Woodstock College, c. 1907.
(Mrs. Helen Rutherford)

Figure 32: Hazel Rutherford, c. 1905.
(Mrs. Hazel McCuaig)

Figure 33: The Rutherford Block (Dominion Bank Building), c. 1908.
(Glenbow-Alberta Institute, NA-1328-716)

Figure 34: Cottage built for Premier Rutherford at Banff in 1908.
(Historic Sites Service)

CHAPTER III

THE RAILWAY CRISIS (1910)

Rutherford emerged from the 1909 election leading another formidable majority in the Legislative Assembly that clearly reflected the broad popular support he and his government enjoyed. The token opposition did, of course, include the redoubtable R. B. Bennett, easily the strongest orator and debater of the time. But against the swarm of thirty-seven Liberals in the government benches, what threat could he pose?

An overwhelming government majority is, however, not without its dangers. Unrestrained by an effective opposition, divisive forces such as parochial preoccupations, conflicting views, and frustrated ambitions can shatter the unity of a large government camp—unless strong leadership is present. As early as 1906 Rutherford had lightly remarked that a good leader can manage a large following, implying that he was such a leader.[1] But now his followers were even more numerous: all had constituents to satisfy and some were eager to share in the executive power. Rutherford did in fact add one member to his Executive Council in October 1909. Two members of his original cabinet were replaced: DeVeber, minister without portfolio, had been appointed to the Senate in 1906, and Finlay, the minister of agriculture, resigned in 1909 on account of poor health. The three new ministers were young and able. Duncan Marshall became the new minister of agriculture and provincial secretary. William Buchanan and Prosper Lessard were not given specific portfolios, but rumour suggested that Buchanan would head a new department of municipal affairs.[2] Meanwhile, Rutherford had added yet another portfolio to his own considerable responsibilities, the Ministry of Railways. He still carried as much of the executive burden as the rest of his cabinet combined. His zeal for hard work made him a leader reluctant to delegate responsibility, who concentrated power in his own hands and left little for his followers to do.

After four years in power, Rutherford had demonstrated his political leadership qualities and was found wanting. Even his warmest admirers acknowledged that he was a poor speaker who inspired no one. His nonpartisanship alienated him from his Liberal colleagues in Alberta and Ottawa, while his inability to share and delegate authority alienated him from his followers in the Legislature. Rather than minimizing regional rivalries such as that between Edmonton and Calgary, he fanned the flames of regionalism by personally locating the university in his own constituency. Rather than addressing the tensions within the Liberal party, he seemed unaware of them, perhaps too preoccupied by his many responsibilities. His own decent and upstanding character and his conviction that good would prevail perhaps blinded him to baser qualities in men. In short, Rutherford was an apolitical politician. His often-expressed reluctance to enter the political arena probably stemmed from his own awareness of this.

Signs of discontent within his ranks were apparent by 1910. Cushing, for example, had been particularly offended by Rutherford's choice of Strathcona for the university, as were Calgary Liberals generally. Only five days before the session began, Cushing testily wrote to Rutherford:

> I enclose another letter regarding payment of [Normal] school site at Calgary. It is now four years since you sent me to Calgary to make this purchase. Is it possible to have amount paid at once?[3]

Cushing had not appreciated being badgered for payment by the public school board in Calgary, where his political credibility was all-important.

Only the summer before, J.R. Boyle, the Liberal M.L.A. for Sturgeon, had written to Rutherford demanding to know why there were no funds in the budget for roads in his constituency.

> I would be glad to know at as early a date as possible why the government has taken this action, in order that I may be in a position to take what stand appears to me proper under the circumstances.[4]

Boyle was understandably concerned about his constituents, and was relieved to learn afterwards that some money would be available for roads in his area. A capable lawyer, Boyle considered himself cabinet material, and it was later rumoured that Rutherford's appointment of Marshall to the agriculture portfolio came as a personal disappointment to him.[5]

Thus, as the session began in 1910, the public could not know that the real opposition to Rutherford's government lay on the Liberal side of the house, and the issue that would bring the "insurgents" into the open would be Rutherford's railway programme, the principal plank in his 1909 election platform. As early as January 1910, a rumour began circulating predicting Cushing's imminent resignation from the government. Cushing acknowledged the rumour, replying, "I have not yet had any intimation that I am not wanted in the cabinet."[6] On the surface, however, it looked like another session of business as usual.

Bennett and Boyle initiated the crisis on the opening day of the session by giving notice of questions regarding railways, particularly the Alberta and Great Waterways Railway, whose bonds had been guaranteed by the province. This company had been incorporated to construct a line from Edmonton to Fort McMurray via Lac la Biche. The legislation permitting the government to guarantee its bonds for 350 miles (563 kilometers) at $20,000 a mile, and for $400,000 for a terminal at Edmonton, had been passed in the 1909 session without difficulty. The principals in the company were William and Bertrand Clarke, Kansas City bankers, and William Bain, a Winnipeg accountant.[7] On 7 October 1909 the agreement between the province and the A. & G.W. Railway had been signed, and the order-in-council approving and ordering the agreement passed.[8] A month later the premier announced that the A. & G.W. bond issue had been sold on the London market by J. Pierpont Morgan and Company at a premium of 110, that is, at 10 per cent above par.

The questions posed by Bennett and Boyle were routinely answered on 15 February by Railways Minister Rutherford. He revealed that to date only five and a half miles (nine kilometers) of the line had been graded and no steel had been laid; that the government was aware of only $50,000 paid-up capital in the company; and that the proceeds from the sale of bonds, $7,400,000, were now deposited in three Edmonton banks and earning interest at 3.5 per cent.[9]

Meanwhile, the rumour persisted that Public Works Minister Cushing, who happened to be absent from the assembly with a cold, had resigned. On 17 February Rutherford finally confirmed the rumour by reading Cushing's letter of resignation from the cabinet, dated three days earlier. Cushing was not in accord with Rutherford on several matters, it read, but specifically he was resigning because he felt that the A.&G.W. bond guarantee, arranged without his knowledge or consent, utterly failed to protect the interests of the people of Alberta.[10] Rutherford accepted the resignation with hearty regret, and expressed complete surprise at any disagreement and astonishment that Cushing could have forgotten his involvement in the A. & G.W. arrangements.[11]

By now the A. & G.W. issue was quickly becoming a provincial obsession, attracting not only packed galleries in the chamber, but massive newspaper coverage as well. On 21 February Boyle gave notice of a resolution to expropriate the rights of the A. & G. W. Railway and have the line built by a commission. In his long preamble he cited the company's inadequate paid-up capital, the failure of the government to make its own estimate of the cost of the line, the exorbitant amount of the guarantee, and the lack of adequate construction standards. In short, he accused the government of failing to take reasonable precautions to protect the public interest. His resolution amounted to a motion of non-confidence.[12]

In the debate that followed, Cushing, now a backbencher, declared that he had been absent from the critical cabinet meeting of 7 October. Rutherford claimed that Cushing had been present, and defended the A.&G. W. agreement at considerable length, concluding that

[f]rom what I have observed and learned within the last few days I have almost arrived at the conclusion that there is a nest of traitors in the Liberal camp in Alberta. It is not a large nest. I don't couple the name of the ex-minister of public works with that nest . . . but I think that he has been misled—he has been duped. If left to his own calm judgement he would still be an honoured and honourable member of my cabinet.[13]

The debate continued for nearly a week and climaxed on 2 March with a five-hour oration by R. B. Bennett in which he dissected the A. & G. W. agreement and heaped scorn and suspicion on the government. He made much of the fact that although Alberta received $7,400,000 (par) for the sale of the bonds, the Morgan Company had realized a premium of $740,000 when it sold them at 110 on the open market. Thus had the Rutherford government enabled "a gang of exploiters and a crowd of speculators to use this province's credit for their personal ends."[14] An amendment to Boyle's resolution proposed that certain safeguards be written into the A. & G.W. agreement; as amended, the resolution was acceptable to the government, and in the vote on 3 March it was sustained twenty-three to fifteen. Twelve Liberal insurgents, including Cushing and Boyle, voted against the government.[15]

The crisis was renewed on 9 March when Rutherford gave notice of a resolution to establish a railway board, which would control the payment of money to railway companies whose bonds had been guaranteed by the province. A proposed member of this board, John Stocks, the deputy minister of public works, announced publicly that he would not be party to a "whitewash" of the A. & G.W. transaction, which he considered to be utterly wrong. That same day Attorney-General Cross submitted his resignation from cabinet, and in quick succession came the resignations of his deputy, S. B. Woods, and of W. A. Buchanan, minister without portfolio. In fact, the situation was not as serious as it appeared. Cross resigned simply because he had learned that Rutherford had persuaded Cushing to re-enter the cabinet; when this subsequently proved false, he withdrew his resignation. Woods had been offered a better job. Only Buchanan wished to be free to express his doubts concerning the A. & G.W. deal.[16] On 10 March Rutherford and Lessard alone occupied the ministerial front bench, but the following day Cross rejoined them. A surprise motion of non-confidence was defeated twenty to seventeen; but two more Liberals had joined the insurgents.

On 14 March the beleaguered premier gave notice of a resolution to appoint a royal commission to enquire whether any members of the government or the legislature had an interest in the organization of the A. & G.W. Railway, its agreement with the province, or the guarantee and sale of its bonds. The commissioners would be three justices of the Alberta Supreme Court: D. L. Scott, H. Harvey, and N. D. Beck. Their findings, it was hoped, would resolve the current allegations that certain members of the legislature, including the premier, had personally profited from the A. & G.W. deal. The resolution establishing the commission was passed unanimously, but not before another resolution deploring the alleged stripping of the A. & G. W. files was narrowly defeated.[17] On 19 March the assembly adjourned until 26 May, when it would convene to consider the commission's findings. Two weeks later Rutherford wrote to a friend in Brandon, Manitoba:

> I appreciate very much your reference to the trouble I have been having recently, but I fully expect I shall come out on top as a result of the investigation of the Royal Commission.

> I quite appreciate that I had too many supporters, and have expected trouble some time, in a general way, but I did not expect it to come exactly when and in the form it did. However, I think that perhaps some people have suffered more than I have.[18]

Meanwhile, the commission had begun its sittings; as the evidence was heard the newspapers reported it fully to an eager public. But the key witness, W. R. Clarke, president of the A. & G. W. Railway, refused to appear, and his refusal cost Rutherford dearly in public confidence. Within Liberal ranks too, confidence in Rutherford had been shattered by his apparent bungling of the railway contract and his perceived inability to lead the party, let the royal commission find what it might. Lieutenant-Governor Bulyea, who privately considered the A. & G. W. agreement "insane," had come to view Rutherford as a liability to the party, an opinion he expressed to Laurier.[19] Though Rutherford and Cross still had supporters in the assembly, the insurgents wanted Cushing as premier. During the crisis in the house, Senator Talbot, president of the Liberal Association of Alberta, arrived from Ottawa and was soon won over to Bulyea's view that a new government was essential if the Liberals were to retain control. The choice of a new premier, made apparently by Bulyea, Talbot, and Laurier,[20] fell on the chief justice of Alberta, Arthur L. Sifton. As a prominent Liberal remote from the warring factions, it was hoped that he might restore party unity and public confidence.

Under pressure now from even his most ardent supporters, Rutherford gave his resignation to Bulyea on the morning of 26 May, a few hours before the Legislative Assembly reconvened:

> Owing to the dissensions in the ranks of the Liberal party in the Legislature, I have considered it advisable in the interests of the Liberal party of Alberta to tender my resignation as Premier.[21]

The Lieutenant-Governor thereupon announced to the legislature that he had accepted Premier Rutherford's resignation and had called on Sifton to form a government. Bulyea then prorogued the troubled first session of Alberta's second legislature until it could be recalled by the new Premier, a move attacked by the Conservatives as unconstitutional.[22]

The royal commission finally adjourned on 6 July 1910, two months after Rutherford's resignation. By this time it had accumulated 3,225 pages of evidence and 255 exhibits.[23] Its findings did not become public until November 1910 when the 58-page report was tabled in the legislature. Judges Scott and Harvey submitted a majority report; Judge Beck, who had reached somewhat different conclusions from the evidence, submitted a minority report. The majority report ended on an inconclusive note:

> [T]he fact that intelligent men [Rutherford and Cross] acting as trustees make an agreement with a stranger [Clarke] for work to be done by him, and make concessions vastly in excess of what were asked by others for the same work, and of what are granted to others for similar work, and with absolutely no knowledge of the cost of the work to be done other than that offered by the other party to the contract, may reasonably give rise to the suspicion that they have been actuated by some motive other than regard for the interests it was their duty to protect. . . . [T]hat motive is personal interest. Many of the facts and circumstances related are consistent with such a conclusion. But the facts are consistent with other conclusions, and in addition to that fact, direct testimony is given by both Dr. Rutherford and Mr. Cross explicitly denying any personal interest whatever. . . . As there is room for doubt that the inference of personal interest is the only reasonable inference to be drawn from the circumstances related, and in view of the positive denial, it can only be said that, in the opinion of your commissioners, the evidence does not warrant the finding that there was or is any such personal interest on the part of Dr. Rutherford or Mr. Cross.[24]

The evidence in the majority report does warrant, however, the conclusion that Rutherford and Cross displayed negligence and gullibility in their handling of the A. & G.W. business.[25]

Judge Beck's conclusions, on the other hand, were anything but indecisive:

> These explanations [of Rutherford and Cross] fully satisfied me that, though in some instances the wisdom of their course may be doubtful, their motives and intentions were honest. . . . In my opinion the imputations thrown upon them have been disproved.[26]

Given this lack of unanimity and the indecisiveness of the majority report, the findings were open to interpretation by press, public, and historians alike, and an absolute

SIC VOS VON VOBIS.
"Well, what do you know about that?"
Hamlet, Act V, Scene II

Figure 35: Aftermath of the railway crisis seen by the *Calgary Eye Opener,* 18 June 1910.
(Glenbow-Alberta Institute)

consensus on the verdict remains elusive.[27] While the suspicion of corruption on the part of Rutherford and Cross was not confirmed, their failure to protect the public interest was amply demonstrated. The *Edmonton Journal* editorialized that "there is nothing to show that the deal was corrupt, but it was almost childishly foolish."[28] On the front page, however, the *Journal* displayed Conservative M.L.A. George Hoadley's distinction between verdicts of "not guilty" and "not proven"; for Hoadley, at least, two of the commissioners had reached the latter, less decisive conclusion.[29]

Unlike Rutherford, Cross did not remain a casualty. In 1912 he was again attorney-general, and, thanks to his large Edmonton following, he was also one of the few Liberals to survive the 1921 election when the United Farmers of Alberta drove the Liberals from power.

Near the end of the second session of the legislature, on 14 December 1910, one of Rutherford's Liberal followers, M.L.A. Alwyn Bramley-Moore, moved that the house express its confidence in the integrity of the former Rutherford administration in view of the findings of the royal commission. The motion was seconded by W. F. Puffer, the member for Lacombe. Following a long silence, Rutherford rose and said that the motion was unnecessary and that he was willing to stand by his record. The Speaker declared the motion out of order, and in withdrawing it, Bramley-Moore declared that he had been motivated by the many members of the house who wanted to be on record as having confidence in the integrity of the former government.[30]

Rutherford was to remain in the political arena for only three more years. While his downfall can clearly be attributed to the central role he played in arranging the dubious A. & G.W. agreement, he also appears to have been a ready victim in a struggle for power among members of the Liberal party, who used the agreement as a means of realizing their ambitions. In spite of the powerful majorities he commanded in the legislature, Rutherford was not regarded as a strong leader by the Liberal hierarchy, not sufficiently aggressive, articulate, or partisan to fight it out with the Conservatives if the need arose.[31] Various assessments of Rutherford by both his friends and opponents reveal his political vulnerability. In 1905 his friend and admirer, J. Hamilton McDonald, editor of the *Strathcona Plaindealer*, wrote:

> His modesty and retiring disposition are too well known to require comment and it is well known that from the beginning of his public career to the present time Mr. Rutherford has been pushed into positions of political prominence by his friends who recognize his qualifications.[32]

W. A. Griesbach, recalling his own part in the 1905 election as a Conservative candidate in Edmonton, mentions that

> [t]he Cabinet Ministers were a group of amicable nobodies. Premier Rutherford was, I think, a pretty sound man, somewhat out of his depth.[33]

R. B. Bennett, who later became Rutherford's friend, is reported to have made a similar observation: "an honest man, but over his head in politics."[34] In his biography of Dr. Tory, E. A. Corbett speaks of Rutherford in the same vein:

> The Prime Minister, Dr. A. C. Rutherford, was a gentleman of the old school, and not equipped by experience or temperament for the rough and tumble of western politics.[35]

And these views were echoed recently by Rutherford's daughter, Mrs. Hazel McCuaig:

> I never thought of him as a politician. I think other people pushed him; he didn't seem to push himself very much. I sometimes wonder how he got where he did.[36]

Nevertheless, Rutherford felt he had been betrayed by a "nest of traitors," and the tributes he received after stepping down must have brought him some comfort. Two days after he resigned, Bob Edwards, the irreverent editor of the *Eye Opener*, wrote Rutherford from Winnipeg:

Just a line to wish you all sorts of prosperity in the future, and good luck. You may safely congratulate yourself on having given Alberta a good clean government and on having come out of this *intentionally* irritating investigation with your honour untarnished. In Winnipeg, where the railway deal has been much discussed, there have been nothing but words of commendation of yourself and of your administration of affairs in the province.... [T]here seems to be general satisfaction that you all have personally come out of it with clean hands. I thought you might like to know this.[37]

The premier of Ontario, J. P. Whitney, wrote Rutherford in June 1910:

No doubt the events of the last few months have been more or less unpleasant to you, but I write as one friend to another to assure you that all those who know you have the same regard for you today as before your troubles commenced.... There is no cloud upon your personal honour, and after all, that is what is important.[38]

But honour and integrity do not guarantee survival in political life. Gentleman and political innocent that he was, Rutherford allowed himself to be manipulated by less scrupulous men and, almost as passively as he had acquired it, let the power of high office slip away.

CHAPTER IV

THE POLITICAL WILDERNESS
(1910–1913 and 1921)

Lieutenant-Governor Bulyea opened the second session of Alberta's second legislature on 10 November 1910 in the Terrace Building. He had just been appointed to his second term as lieutenant-governor, a reward, it was said, for his handling of the government crisis earlier in the year.[1] Premier Sifton now headed the large Liberal force in the assembly; Rutherford, Cross, and Cushing had all been relegated to the back benches. On the other side of the house, the small opposition was now officially led by Edward Michener of Red Deer. R. B. Bennett was present for this and the following session, but would resign in 1911 to begin his career in federal politics.

The Liberal ranks were still divided between the Rutherford-Cross faction on the one hand and the followers of Sifton and Cushing on the other; the divisive railway issue was yet to be resolved. In July 1910, when the A. & G.W. Railway had defaulted on payment of interest on its bonds, the Sifton government had paid it. Now Sifton introduced legislation to transfer the $7,400,000 in bond proceeds to the credit of the province, a move intended to free the government from the ill-fated A. & G.W. agreement and restore party unity. Sifton's bill immediately produced opposition both within and outside the legislature. The Rutherford-Cross faction attacked it as an abandonment of northern development, while the Conservatives branded it as confiscatory legislation that would ruin the standing of Alberta in world money markets and lead to endless litigation. The Sifton forces nevertheless passed the bill by a margin of twenty-five to fourteen,[2] but the breach in the Liberal ranks remained. In any case the legislation failed to achieve its purpose: the banks refused to pay the money over to the province. The Sifton government launched legal proceedings, and two years

67

Figure 36: A.C. Rutherford School, c. 1920.
(Rutherford School Archives)

later, in January 1913, the Privy Council decided in favour of the banks. Meanwhile, the Sifton government was financially hamstrung, not knowing if it would eventually have access to the money or not.

Earlier in the session, Liberal M.L.A. Bramley-Moore (Lloydminster) introduced a resolution requesting that the Laurier government give Alberta control of its lands and resources. Premier Sifton expressed sympathy for the motion but asked that it be withdrawn, declaring that control of resources could be accomplished only by negotiation, which he intended to pursue. The resolution was finally amended to express the members' approval and encouragement of such negotiations, and in this tactful guise it received the unanimous approval of the house.[3] Thus, having acquiesced for five years to the federal terms of autonomy that provided grants in lieu of lands and resources, the Alberta Liberals were officially prepared to negotiate for full autonomy. The negotiations would drag on for the next twenty years.

Though Rutherford had been unseated as premier, he still had supporters. During the summer of 1910 when Laurier visited the West, Rutherford left his cottage at Banff to be present at the welcoming celebrations in Strathcona. Cross apparently used the occasion to urge on Laurier a senate appointment for Rutherford, later informing the ex-premier: "I think things will turn out alright as far as you are concerned."[4] The senate appointment never materialized,[5] although Rutherford was made a King's Counsel in March 1913,[6] a designation he had sought as early as 1905.[7] In October 1910 he was invited to open the Stettler fair, and at the banquet given there in his honour, he received high tributes for his work as premier and minister of railways.[8]

In Strathcona, a new school under construction was named Alexander Rutherford.[9] Nor were Rutherford's abilities and experience ignored in the legislature: he was a member of several standing committees, including those for legal bills, public accounts, municipal law, and miscellaneous private bills.[10]

In early February 1911 the Rutherfords moved into their handsome new residence in the university area,[11] where they were to live for the next thirty years. A month later Rutherford was elected to the university senate for a five-year term. As premier, he had been an ex officio member of the original senate, but his resignation from the government also removed him from the governing body of the university. It is noteworthy that Rutherford, already known as the "father of the university," easily topped the poll in the 1911 senate elections.[12]

Following a two-month trip to Europe in the spring of 1911,[13] Rutherford became embroiled in the 1911 federal election campaign that led to the defeat of the Laurier regime that September. Frank Oliver, minister of the interior and member of Parliament for Edmonton, had recently lost a great deal of support in Alberta. Long absences in Ottawa and allegations of graft had contributed to this loss, but in some quarters of the Alberta Liberal party the main issue was the part Oliver was alleged to have played in the downfall of the Rutherford administration. During the A. & G.W. crisis, Oliver's newspaper, the *Edmonton Bulletin*, took the side of the insurgents. Oliver claimed that because he was in Ottawa he had given his editor a free hand in the issue, but his denial of complicity made little headway against the charge that he had personally conspired to unseat Rutherford and Cross and delay northern railway development.[14] There had long been bad blood between Oliver and Cross, and Rutherford's warm association with Cross could not have endeared him to Oliver.[15] Thus in early August 1911, a delegation of Cross-Rutherford Liberals approached Rutherford asking him to contest the Edmonton riding against Oliver in the forthcoming federal election. On 8 August Rutherford announced his decision to allow his name to stand, and at a Liberal convention held in Edmonton on 16 August he was unanimously nominated to contest the federal seat.[16] Rutherford declared himself a supporter of Reciprocity, a reciprocal reduction of duties on goods traded between Canada and the United States, and a major plank in the federal Liberal platform. But he was truly preoccupied with more local issues: Alberta's control of its lands and resources, and northern railway development.[17]

The convention also passed resolutions condemning Oliver for his failure to explain his large bank account and for his opposition to the Rutherford railway policy.[18] Oliver had termed the convention "bogus," and awaited the results of another Liberal nominating convention scheduled for September.[19] Meanwhile, Rutherford challenged Oliver to have his bank account inspected by a supreme court judge.[20] It was subsequently rumoured that Oliver was trying to buy Rutherford off with the promise of a judgeship.[21]

Then, on 24 August, the *Edmonton Bulletin* baldly announced that Rutherford had withdrawn from the contest. The *Strathcona Plaindealer* later suggested that he had backed out when asked to contribute $15,000 towards his campaign fund.[22] Rutherford's own explanation was different:

> To the Liberals of the Edmonton Electoral District
>
> Gentlemen. — Owing to three candidates being in the field for election in the Edmonton Electoral District and as the Reciprocity issue is paramount in the election throughout Canada, I have decided to retire from the contest.
>
> I am grateful to the Liberals for their nomination at a regularly constituted convention, and for many assurances of support from all parts of the District.
>
> A.C. Rutherford[23]

The "three candidates" appear to have been Rutherford and Oliver for the Liberals and W. A. Griesbach for the Conservatives. Rutherford may have thought that, because of his great popularity with both Liberals and Conservatives, the Conservatives would not field a candidate once he was nominated, and Oliver would drop out of the race. When neither happened, Rutherford withdrew in order not to jeopardize the success of the Liberals.[24] Oliver was duly nominated and returned in the 21 September election, but lost his interior portfolio with the defeat of the Laurier government.

The third session of the legislature met in December 1911 in the new legislative chamber at the south end of the still unfinished Legislative Building. During this session the Sifton government introduced bills to guarantee the bonds of several new railway lines, including the Edmonton, Dunvegan and British Columbia Railway into the Peace River country, and the Canadian Northern Western Railway to Lac la Biche and Fort McMurray.[25] These bills appeased the Rutherford-Cross faction in the assembly, and the restored unity in Liberal ranks was symbolized by the elevation of both Cross and Boyle to the cabinet, Cross to his former portfolio of attorney-general, Boyle to education.

The fourth and final session of the second legislature convened in February 1913 on the heels of the unfavourable Privy Council decision regarding the A. & G.W. bond money. An opposition amendment to the reply to the speech from the throne, deploring the position in which Alberta had been placed by the "unwise and illegal" legislation of 1910, was supported by Rutherford and one other Liberal.[26] At dissolution in March the $7,400,000 had been lying in Edmonton banks for more than three years and there was still no solution in sight.

The provincial election was called for 17 April. It was to be Rutherford's last campaign, and like his abortive performance in 1911, it would be politically courageous, if not rash.

Early in the campaign Rutherford made it clear that on the central issue of the A. & G.W. Railway he was, and always had been, unalterably opposed to the Sifton policy of confiscation. His position earned him the editorial wrath of the pro-Sifton *Edmonton Bulletin*, which linked Rutherford to the Conservatives as an enemy of the public interest.[27] The most sensational event of the campaign occurred at the South Edmonton Conservative nominating convention on 29 March. A letter from Rutherford to the president of the Conservative convention was read to the delegates. In it the ex-premier said he was opposed to Sifton on the A. & G.W. question; if the Conservatives did not field a candidate in South Edmonton, he himself would campaign anywhere in the province on behalf of Conservative candidates.[28] Coming from the former leader of the Alberta Liberals, this was a bombshell indeed. But Rutherford's offer was declined; although some two dozen Conservative delegates supported him, he was still considered "politically down and out." An untried young candidate named H. H. Crawford was nominated by the convention.29

The southside Liberals held their convention two days later, and some of the delegates were understandably anxious to have an explanation from Rutherford before supporting his nomination. Rutherford was sent for and, as reported by the *Edmonton Bulletin*, the following scenario unfolded:

> [Dr. Rutherford]: "I am glad to meet such an enthusiastic audience of Liberals. I am a Liberal of the Liberals myself, and I stand, and have always stood, for good Liberal principles. Some newspapers made a little flutter . . . about my sending a quite innocent letter which was read at the Conservative convention on Saturday afternoon. I am not ashamed to read that letter if you want to hear it. . . . There is nothing in it which is in the least detrimental to me or to any Liberals in this province."
>
> Dr. Rutherford proceeded to read the letter, but he was interrupted by Mr. Lang, who wanted to know what led up to the letter being written.
>
> Dr. Rutherford: A committee of the Conservative executive called upon me and wanted to know where I stood.
>
> Dr. Rutherford then read the second letter as given above [the *Bulletin* published two versions of the letter]. He went on to say: "The question at issue as referred to in that letter . . . is the solution of the Waterways question. Mr. Sifton brought down his solution in 1910. I opposed it. I did not think he was taking a business-like way of settling the matter. I therefore voted for a want of confidence motion with the government on that question. As you are well aware, not one cent of the proceeds of the sale of the bonds had been used. Every cent was in the bank. Sifton proposed a policy that has been declared illegal by the highest court in the realm. The Privy Council judgement places the province in the same position as it was before, and Sifton ought to have brought down a solution during the recent session, and every good Liberal thinks so, too. Of course, like every good Liberal, if good measures are brought forward by the government returned to power, I will

support them, but you don't expect me to support measures that are not in harmony with good Liberal principles."

"At the session of 1910 I proposed a solution on the floor of the house. I stated that one of the great transcontinental railway companies was prepared to build that road, settle with the bank, assume the bonded indebtedness, and the province would not have lost five cents. It will not be so easy to settle today."

"I want to make it plain that I stand at all times for good sound Liberalism. I was selected at a convention of Liberals in the city of Calgary by a unanimous vote to be the prime minister of this province. I carried two elections almost unanimously, so far as the return of members was concerned, and I need not tell you that the Waterways question was merely an excuse on the part of some members who were returned as my supporters. Other issues entered into the matter entirely outside of the Waterways matter, and there is no difficulty in sizing up what some of them were."

. . . I am no hypocrite. I want to make it plain that I am not running as a Sifton candidate, if you will nominate me in this constituency.

Mr. MacKinnon: Are you running as a Michener candidate?

Dr. Rutherford: I am a good independent candidate, and you can't have a better. I'm a good Liberal, too.

Mr. Herbert: Are you willing to run as a good independent Liberal candidate?

Dr. Rutherford: I have stated that very plainly.

The vote was then taken and after the nomination had been made unanimous, Dr. Rutherford made a brief speech of thanks.[30]

This was all too much for the *Edmonton Journal*, which breathlessly declared:

It is absolutely without parallel in the history of Canada that a former party leader should take the stand that Mr. Rutherford has and be endorsed by the party in his own constituency in so unqualified a manner.[31]

Rutherford and Crawford campaigned vigorously during the next two weeks, while the *Bulletin* continued to condemn both Rutherford and the Conservatives.[32] When the ballots were counted, the Sifton government was sustained, having won thirty-eight seats to the Conservatives' eighteen in an enlarged assembly of fifty-six. But in South Edmonton it was for Crawford that the band played "For He's a Jolly Good Fellow." Rutherford thanked his loyal supporters, attributed his narrow defeat to the many new people swelling South Edmonton's population,[33] and, at the age of fifty-six, concluded a career in political office that had begun eleven years before.

Eight years later, during the 1921 provincial election campaign, Rutherford appeared at a Conservative rally to speak on behalf of the five Conservative candidates seeking election in greater Edmonton. One of the candidates was A. F. Ewing, leader of the Conservative party in Alberta. Another was H. H. Crawford, who had defeated Rutherford in 1913.[34] Rutherford spoke as "a life-long Liberal," but he had no hesitation in condemning the present Liberal administration on two counts: the enormous growth of the provincial debt, and the disorganization of the Liberal party. Both resulted, he said, from "rotten" Liberal administration. Rutherford offered the Liberals a slogan: "Get Rid of the Barnacles and the Boyles."[35] It may be recalled that J. R. Boyle, then attorney-general in the Liberal government, had played a key role in Rutherford's overthrow eleven years before.

The *Edmonton Journal* commented editorially on the spectacle of the first Liberal premier actively supporting Conservative candidates, suggesting that old party lines in Alberta were now completely shattered.[36] The election results a week later bore this out. After sixteen years in power, the Liberals went down to defeat at the hands of the upstart United Farmers of Alberta. The Conservatives were almost completely wiped out, returning only one member. Both Liberals and Conservatives faced a long bleak future in Alberta in both federal and provincial elections.

Rutherford's frustrated political career helped to set Alberta on a unique political course. As a political leader, Rutherford was essentially an Ontario-bred, non-partisan, provincial nationalist, and as such he set himself—and Alberta—on a collision course with the fiercely partisan and centralist preoccupations of the Laurier regime. In Alberta, Rutherford was also in conflict with partisan and parochial Liberals unrestrained by an effective opposition. Rutherford's Ontarian aspirations for Alberta were frustrated by Ottawa: he was denied control of natural resources, a land endowment for the university, loans or guarantees to stimulate railway construction, and was even reproved for the government telephone system. In 1909, having already unveiled his made-in-Alberta railway policy, Rutherford defiantly proclaimed that "the Province must stand before the party," and won another huge majority in the legislature. A year later, his Liberal colleagues in Ottawa and Alberta found the means of discrediting and disowning him in the A.&G.W. Railway agreement.

Disillusioned and alienated, Rutherford remained a "true" Liberal even as he attacked the Liberal establishment on the one hand and offered his support to the Conservatives on the other. As a major participant in federalism and the political system in Alberta during its formative years, Rutherford had been thwarted and ultimately destroyed. Originally an Ontario colonizer, he had come to see himself as a colonial, and Alberta as a colony. He was not alone.

Alwyn Bramley-Moore, the Liberal member from Lloydminster in the second Alberta Legislature, wrote *Canada and Her Colonies or Home Rule for Alberta* in

1911.[37] The book denounced the colonial status of a province deprived of the control of its natural resources by a "foreign" government that regarded the West as "a speculation or investment." Bramley-Moore argued that Ottawa had granted Alberta a limited constitution in 1905. Then

> a great victory was won by the [provincial] Liberal party, and they were the associates of the [federal] party who had framed the constitution. But this action of the electorate confirmed nothing. They were willing to give it a trial.

> ... But as the province grows older, so does a provincial nationality become more in evidence. The settlers, no longer strangers, take a steadily-increasing interest in everything; participation in elections creates a feeling of ownership in the province, and from these newly-aroused feelings is generated a discontent and dissatisfaction at the mutilated and disfigured constitution they have been granted.[38]

A friend and supporter of Rutherford, Bramley-Moore declared in his preface that

> [a]s a member of the Alberta Legislature I could not fail from being deeply influenced by witnessing the total overthrow of the Rutherford government on account of their efforts to open up the northern portions of the province.

> Nothing could have more forcibly brought home to my mind the injustice of a state of affairs by which a Provincial Government assumes the liabilities incident to the development of a vast country while the natural resources of that country are owned and controlled by a foreign Government.[39]

Among suggested avenues of redress, Bramley-Moore included the possibility that Alberta "hoist the flag of independence, which would ipso facto make the province owner of her own resources."[40]

> We are not urging a secession of the West from the East, but we are endeavouring to show that such a result must ensue unless a change in her system of colonial government is made by Canada.[41]

Having witnessed their popular premier's relegation to the political wilderness, Albertans would soon seek redress from federal domination by abandoning the two old-line parties. Just as decisively as they had supported the Liberals, they turned en masse to the United Farmers of Alberta[42] and later to the Social Credit party, while in federal elections they gave their support to the Progressive party and then to Social Credit. But the province's malaise within the federal system, exemplified and nurtured by the first premier, remained a recurring theme.

CHAPTER V

CITIZEN RUTHERFORD (1910 - 1941)

Rutherford's resignation from the premier's office in 1910, and his defeat in the 1913 provincial election, removed a heavy burden of responsibility from his life. No longer subject to the endless demands of the political arena, his last thirty years were more leisurely and self-directed, but, as always, productive.

In 1910, after an absence of five years, he returned to his law practice. The firm of Rutherford, Jamieson and Mode had lost its junior partner in September 1909, when Mode became clerk of the district court at Wetaskiwin.[1] In November 1910 Charles Grant, a student-at-law with the firm, was admitted to the Alberta bar and became the new junior partner in Rutherford, Jamieson and Grant.[2] At the same time the firm opened a branch office in Edmonton in McDougall Court, located on what later became 100 Street opposite the future Macdonald Hotel. Rutherford himself occupied the north side office in the afternoons, but spent the mornings on the south side with his partners in the Imperial Bank Building.[3] The firm remained the solicitors for the City of Strathcona until its amalgamation with Edmonton in early 1912. In 1916 the Edmonton office was relocated to the McLeod Building. In 1917 George H. Steer joined the firm, then known as Rutherford, Jamieson, Grant and Steer until 1920 when Steer left the firm.[4] In 1936 the firm closed the south side office. From 1910 to 1940 Rutherford's partner frequently appeared before the Alberta Supreme Court to argue a variety of cases, but Rutherford himself did not.[5] As the senior partner, however, Rutherford probably helped his partners to work up their cases. As a solicitor, Rutherford appears to have handled legal transactions concerning such matters as contracts, real estate, wills and estates, and incorporation. For example, as the original solicitor for the Great Western Garment Company, he had that company incorporated in 1911.

Figure 37: The City of Strathcona, intersection of Whyte Avenue and First Street
East (now 103 Street), c. 1910.
(Mrs. Hazel McCuaig)

Figure 38: Dr. Rutherford in his law office, Imperial Bank Building, 1911.
(Mrs. Hazel McCuaig)

Figure 39: Imperial Bank Building, 63 and 65 Whyte Avenue, n.d.
(Glenbow-Alberta Institute, NA-1328-713)

Figure 40: Rutherford House, c. 1913.
(Glenbow-Alberta Institute, NA-1328-525)

In the spring of 1910 construction began on Rutherford's new house in the university area. The foundation was completed at precisely the time he submitted his resignation. Work continued through 1910 and the Rutherfords moved into the completed mansion during the first week of February 1911. Two months later Dr. Rutherford left on his second trip to Britain and the continent, this time with his younger sister Jessie.[6] He attended another imperial conference on education in London, and toured Europe. He was invited to attend the coronation of King George V in Westminster Abbey on 22 June, but was forced to return home before the event took place. The following summer, 1912, Rutherford was back in Britain with his daughter Hazel. They attended a royal garden party at Windsor Castle on 18 July and visited ancestral Aberfeldy in Scotland.[7] Mrs. Hazel McCuaig recalls attending many stage plays with her father in London, but the most memorable event for her was seeing the great Pavlova perform in the ballet *Swan Lake.*

During his three trips to London (1907, 1911, 1912), Rutherford visited the prestigious photographic studio of Elliott and Fry at 55 Baker Street, where he sat for several portraits. The photograph published in John Blue's *Alberta Past and Present* (1924) was probably taken in 1907, while the portrait that appeared in A. O. MacRae's *The History of the Province of Alberta* (1912) was likely done in 1911. The latter portrait of Rutherford, seated and sans spectacles, was photographed full length and was apparently the model for two subsequent oil paintings. One was painted by the English portrait artist William Everitt, who may have had Rutherford sit for him in London in 1912. The finished head-and-shoulders portrait hung over the fireplace in the library of Rutherford House until 1940. Eventually acquired by Cecil Rutherford, it was donated by him to the University of Alberta in 1952[8] and is now housed in the university archives. In 1973, following the restoration of Rutherford House, a photographic duplicate of the original was made by the Meisel Photochrome Corporation of Dallas, Texas, for the Provincial Museum of Alberta. This copy now hangs in the house where the original did, unveiled by Mrs. Hazel McCuaig on 11 May 1974, when the house was officially opened to the public. The other oil painting based on the Elliott and Fry portrait now hangs in the legislative building, but is unsigned and undated. In style it resembles a number of other portraits by the Canadian artist Victor A. Long (1866–1938), and indeed it was attributed to Long by the *Edmonton Bulletin* at the time of Rutherford's death.[9] Unlike the Everitt portrait, this one is three-quarters length. Long painted another portrait of Rutherford in 1911, a head-and-shoulders study that is signed and dated, which now hangs at the entrance of the Rutherford North Library, University of Alberta.

Rutherford's concern and enthusiasm for the university did not diminish during his post-political period. As a member of the University Senate from 1911 to 1927, he was intimately involved in the growth and development of the institution he had founded. In 1912 he instituted the Rutherford Gold Medal in English for the senior honours English student with the highest standing,[10] a prize that is still offered by the university. In the afternoon of 9 May 1912 the first graduating class at the university planted a tree on the campus, then walked over to Rutherford House for tea.[11] Thus

Figure 41: Premier A.C. Rutherford,
Elliott and Fry Photog-
raphers, London,
England, 1907.
(Provincial Archives of
Alberta, H73-34-16)

Figure 42: Premier A.C. Rutherford,
Elliott and Fry Photog-
raphers, London, England,
1907.
(Glenbow-Alberta In-
stitute, NA-1514-5)

Figure 43: Dr. A.C. Rutherford, Elliott and Fry Photographers, London, England, 1911.
(University of Alberta Archives, 69-112)

Figure 44: William Everitt
Portrait, 1912, in
University of Alberta
Archives, 74-26.
(Historic Sites
Service, 79R267-12)

Figure 45: Victor A. Long
Portrait, 1911, in
Rutherford North
Library.
(Historic Sites Ser-
vice, 79R267-10)

Figure 46: Victor A. Long
Portrait, n.d., in
Legislative Building.
(Historic Sites
Service, 79R167-6)

began the annual Founder's Day Tea at Rutherford House, a traditional part of convocation exercises at the University of Alberta for the next twenty-six years.[12]

On 21 May 1927 the convocation elected Dr. Rutherford chancellor of the university, an honour he prized above all others.[13] He was re-elected by acclamation to a four-year term of office in three subsequent elections, and held the post until his death in July 1941, just three weeks after the 1941 convocation. As chancellor it was his proud duty to preside at convocation and to admit members of the graduation class to their degrees:

> By virtue of the authority vested in me by the Legislature of this province and with the consent of the Senate of this University, I consent to admit you to the degrees to which you are entitled, and to invest you with all the powers, rights, and privileges pertaining to that degree, and I charge you to use them for the glory of God and the honour of your country.[14]

It has been estimated that Chancellor Rutherford conferred degrees on some five thousand graduants in the course of his fourteen years as titular head of the university.

Figure 47: Chancellor A.C. Rutherford, 1927.
              (University of Alberta Archives)

Figure 48: "The Goal is Reached." Chancellor Rutherford at Convocation, c. 1937. (*Evergreen and Gold* [1938])

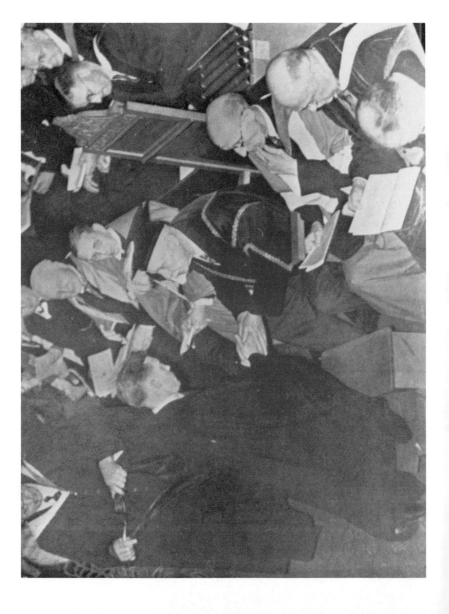

Figure 49: Alexander and Mattie Rutherford in the garden at Rutherford House, c. 1930.
(Mrs. Hazel McCuaig)

For fifteen [*sic*] years he proudly took his place at the head of the solemn convocation parade, to beam comfortingly on some 5,000 nervous graduants who kneeled to lay sweating hands in his during the degree-granting ceremony, or to chat companionably with them as they filed to his imposing mansion across from the arts building to drink tea with him before quitting forever its halls of learning. ... .

. . . Chancellor Rutherford learned to sit tolerant and forebearing when unrepressed engineering students . . . let loose a noisy white rooster in the midst of [one convocation].

Applause was never louder . . . when Leonard W. Brockington, present to receive an honorary degree, said of the beaming chancellor, "Time has dealt so gently and graciously with Dr. Rutherford because he has dealt so graciously and gently with his fellow men."[15]

Students were frequent visitors at Rutherford House, for Rutherford had one of the finest Canadiana collections in western Canada. He had begun collecting books early in life, and by the time he moved into his new house his library had achieved a certain fame. During his post-political period he turned to book collecting with renewed enthusiasm, so that even his commodious library shelves could no longer accommodate the vast collection. His books eventually overflowed into the den, the maid's sitting room, and even into the garage. His family remember him typically sitting in the library with a new book catalogue, perhaps from the British Museum, carefully perusing it and checking off the books he wanted to order.[16] He concentrated on Canadiana, biography, fiction and poetry, travel and government documents, and especially western Canadian history. Rutherford knew his library intimately:

Father may not have read every one of his books, but he had a very good idea of the contents of all of them, and he knew exactly where each one was to be found on the shelves.[17]

He generously threw his library open to students at the university and to others:

He was a lover of books, and had acquired a library of Canadiana, which had few peers, among private collections. Not only had he the library, but he knew his books. Many students sought him to obtain assistance in some phase of Canadian studies. He could give the necessary references, and he could usually supply the necessary material out of his wealth of books and pamphlets and documents.[18]

Following Dr. Rutherford's death in 1941, his vast library was inherited by his son and daughter, Cecil Rutherford and Mrs. Hazel McCuaig. When the Rutherford estate was settled in 1950, Mrs. McCuaig donated her share of the Canadiana collection to the University of Alberta library. The donation comprised some 1,500 titles and was described in 1967 as "still the most important rare collection in the Library."[19] In 1950 the library also acquired Cecil's share of his father's collection for $7,000.[20] Thus, Rutherford's

> extensive collection of early books and documents related to Western Canada . . . eventually became the nucleus of the outstanding Western Canadian History Library in the University. His dedication to Western Canadian History further established the University of Alberta as the main centre of Western Canadian history studies in the nation.[21]

It may be recalled that Rutherford himself made generous donations to the university library as early as 1908, and was active in acquiring government publications for the library. He also personally introduced the bill to establish public libraries in the province in 1907. Rutherford truly demonstrated that books were his "good friends."

Yet he was also a practical man of affairs. At various times he was president of the Edmonton Mortgage Corporation, and vice-president of the Great Western Garment Company.[22] He was a director of the Canada National Fire Insurance Company, the Imperial Canadian Trust Company, the Great West Permanent Loan Company,[23] and the Monarch Life Assurance Company. And he held shares in the Pioneers' Fire Insurance Company.[24]

The Great Western Garment Company (G.W.G.) incorporated in 1911, one of Rutherford's more enduring business ventures, was an immediate, resounding success. Rutherford was a co-founder and major shareholder in the venture. Besides being the firm's original vice-president, Rutherford was its original solicitor. The company began production of overalls with eight seamstresses in a small Edmonton factory, but quadrupled its work force within a year as the demand for its quality work clothing grew. Its workers were unionized from the beginning and were the first garment workers in North America to enjoy an eight-hour workday. The G.W.G. trademark remains a household word across the country more than seventy-five years after Rutherford invested nearly $10,000 in the dream.[25]

From 1912 to 1915 two students-at-law articled with Rutherford's law firm of Rutherford, Jamieson and Grant. One was Rutherford's son Cecil who had attended the University of Alberta from 1908 to 1910; the other, Stanley Harwood McCuaig, was a graduate from Queen's University. World War I interrupted the law career of both. It was only after serving overseas that they were admitted to the Alberta bar in 1919. In 1923 both became partners in the expanded firm of Rutherford, Jamieson, Rutherford and McCuaig, so named as a result of Grant's departure. Then, after twenty-six years as Rutherford's partner, F. C. Jamieson established his own practice in 1925. The firm of Rutherford, Rutherford and McCuaig continued until 1939 when McCuaig, who had married Rutherford's daughter Hazel in 1919, also set up on his own. During the last two years of his life, Rutherford's firm was known as Rutherford, Rutherford and Newton (Gordon J.).[26]

Dr. Rutherford's post-political years were amply filled with institutional activities. He remained a deacon in his church until an advanced age and was still a church trustee at the time of his death.[27] In 1913 he became a member of the Y.W.C.A. advisory board and remained on the board until his death.[28] In March 1914, when the Benevolent and Protective Order of Elks instituted a lodge in Edmonton, Rutherford was chosen as its first exalted ruler. Later that year, at a grand lodge session in Moose Jaw, Saskatchewan, Rutherford was elected grand exalted ruler of the Elk Order of Canada, a position he held until 1917. Two years later he was granted honorary life membership in the grand lodge.[29] From 1915 to 1918 he was president of the St. Andrew's Society,[30] for which he had personally introduced the incorporation bill in the legislature in 1906. From 1916 to 1918 he was Alberta director of the National Service Commission, the body responsible for recruitment during World War I.[31] In 1916 he was appointed honorary colonel of the 194th Highland Battalion, Canadian Expeditionary Force.[32] He personally donated the battalion's colours, which Mrs. Rutherford presented in a ceremony on 27 May 1916. The St. Andrew's Society raised the money for the battalion's pipes and drums.[33] Following the war he was a member of the Loan Advisory Committee of the Soldier Settlement Board.[34]

In 1919 Rutherford was elected president of the Alberta Historical Society, a position he held continuously until 1941.[35] His government had passed the act incorporating the society as early as 1907. Rutherford's knowledge and keen interest in western Canadian history is further reflected by his contribution of the foreword to the 1939 posthumous publication of *The Law Marches West*, a history of the North-West Mounted Police written by one of its original members, Sir Cecil Denny. As an example of Rutherford's unvarnished writing style, the conclusion of the foreword is typical:

> I have read the manuscript of this book, The Law Marches West, by Sir Cecil Denny. It is a most interesting work. It is a worth-while authentic addition to the historical works relating to the history of the great North-West of Canada, and in particular of the province of Alberta.[36]

In 1922 he was elected president of the McGill University Alumni Association of Alberta.[37] Rutherford was long active in the Edmonton branch of the Canadian Authors' Association and had been honorary president of the organization for many years at the time of his death.[38] In their later years the Rutherfords were members of the Northern Alberta Pioneers and Old-Timers Association.[39] Dr. Rutherford was a Fellow of the British Association for the Advancement of Science, and of the Royal Colonial Institute of London.[40] He also remained an active Mason until his death.

Recognition of Rutherford's generous service in so many fields came not only in the honorary offices bestowed on him. In 1923 Dr. and Mrs. E. K. Broadus dedicated their *Anthology of Canadian Prose and Verse* to him:

> To Alexander Cameron Rutherford, who played an honourable part in the upbuilding of the West, this book is affectionately dedicated.[41]

McGill University bestowed on him his fourth honorary LL.D. degree in 1931, fifty years after his graduation from that institution. Rutherford was one of ten thousand Canadians to receive a jubilee medal commemorating the twenty-fifth anniversary of the coronation of King George V.[42] When Dr. and Mrs. Rutherford celebrated their golden wedding anniversary on 19 December 1938, tributes poured in from friends and associates all over Canada.[43]

Despite a slight bronchial weakness, Rutherford was a robust man for most of his life. He occasionally consumed alcohol in social settings outside his home, and smoked a cigar or a pipe now and then. In December 1920 he and Cecil became charter members of the Mayfair Golf and Country Club:[44] at age sixty-four Dr. Rutherford had discovered golf! This game replaced tennis, which he had played until his late fifties. He remained a golfer for the next twenty years, winning a number of prizes including the low score medal in an inter-faculty tournament in 1929. His golfing was not powerful, but it was accurate. In his later years he was afflicted with diabetes, and Mrs. Rutherford carefully monitored his sugar intake. When he was out of town and beyond her supervision, he was known to sometimes treat himself to the prohibited sweets. Fully aware, however, that his wife worried about him, Rutherford would assure her in letters and postcards that he wasn't sick yet.[45]

Diabetes may have contributed to a severe stroke he suffered in 1938 that left him paralysed and speechless. With characteristic determination, he learned to walk again. With the help of a grade one reader, he also regained his speech.[46] Mrs. Rutherford faced a different ordeal: cancer finally claimed her on 13 September 1940 at the age of seventy-four. On 11 June 1941, three weeks after presiding at convocation and only a week after playing golf with his friend J. C. Bowen,[47] Rutherford was in an Edmonton hospital for observation and insulin treatment. Having gotten out of bed to read the newspapers, he became dizzy, returned to bed, and moments later died of a heart attack. He was eighty-four.[48] They are buried together in Mount Pleasant Cemetery with their daughter Marjorie, and Cecil who died in 1957.

The last few weeks of Rutherford's life were unfortunately darkened by the bizarre events surrounding the final convocation at which he presided on 19 May 1941.[49] In February 1941 the university's Senate Committee of Honorary Degrees agreed that an honorary LL.D. degree should be conferred on Premier William Aberhart in recognition of his many contributions to education in Alberta. University president W. A. R. Kerr extended the invitation to the premier, inviting him to deliver the convocation address as well. Premier Aberhart accepted both honours. Then on 12 May 1941, a week prior to convocation, the full University Senate met and, among other things, voted unanimously against the recommended honorary degree for Aberhart. This action, which the *Edmonton Bulletin* termed "a miserable trick" by men "full of malice,"[50] was particularly humiliating for President Kerr, who submitted his resignation the day after convocation. Although Chancellor Rutherford presided over the troubled convocation, his undeserved mortification undoubtedly accompanied him to the grave.

CHAPTER VI

ACHNACARRY: RUTHERFORD'S HOUSE

B y 1908, three years after he had become premier, Rutherford was considering the erection of a new house more in keeping with his high public office. He and his family had now lived for thirteen years in the considerably enlarged original house on 104 Street. As the owner of attractive property along the east side of Mill Creek (today's Bonnie Doon district), he had already made plans to build there when Laurent Garneau put his subdivision on the market.

Garneau was the owner of river lot seven in the western suburbs of the City of Strathcona.[1] In the spring of 1909 he had a five-block subdivision surveyed in the northwest corner of his property adjoining river lot five, the university land. The subdivision consisted mostly of 33-by-132-foot (10-by-40-metre) lots, with three larger triangular lots created by the angle of Saskatchewan Avenue (now Saskatchewan Drive). The largest of these triangular parcels of land, lot twelve in block 183, contained 1.3 acres (0.5 hectares).[2] On 29 May 1909 Alexander Cameron Rutherford, described in the certificate of title as "a gentleman of Strathcona," became the owner of "an estate in fee simple of and in lot twelve in block 183 of a subdivision of part of river lot 7 in the said City of Strathcona."[3]

Because there was then no bridge across Mill Creek and access to the east side of the ravine was difficult, Rutherford decided to build on the Garneau site; no doubt its proximity to the future university was a factor as well. By October 1909 plans for a two-storey mansion had been prepared by the Strathcona firm of A. G. Wilson and D. E. Herrald, British-trained architects and civil engineers.[4] About the end of October, the Strathcona contractors James Smith and J. T. Radford completed the basement excavation on lot 12.[5] Thomas Richards, a Strathcona building contractor and master

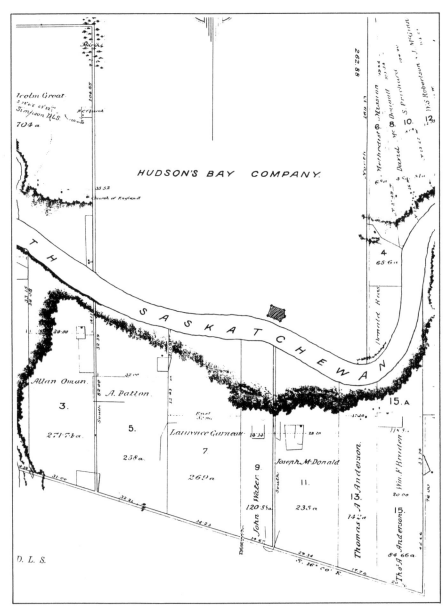

Figure 50: Part of Plan of Edmonton Settlement, N.W.T., 1883.
          (Land Titles Office, Edmonton)

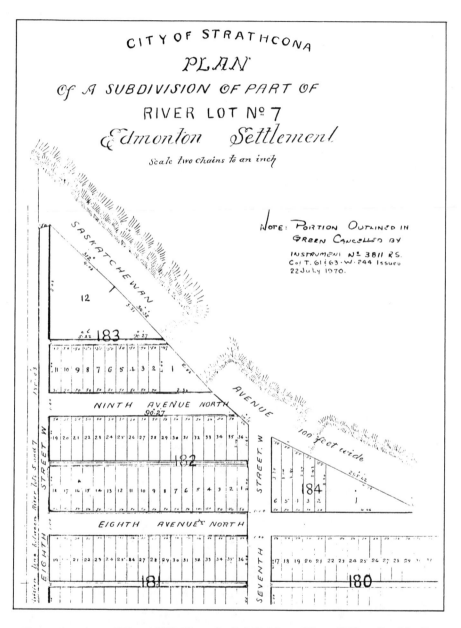

Figure 51: Part of Plan 443X, Plan of a Subdivision of Part of River Lot No. 7, 1909.
(Land Titles Office, Edmonton)

Figure 52: Rutherford House under construction, 1910.
Walter Pierce house to the right, Simpson barn to the left.
(University of Alberta Archives, 76-25-338)

Figure 53: Rutherford House, c. 1913. The side porch is not yet enclosed.
(Glenbow-Alberta Institute, NC-6-1028)

bricklayer, then began construction of the house in the spring of 1910.[6] By the end of May 1910, coinciding with Rutherford's resignation from office, the foundation was poured. Work continued through 1910 on the brick and stone structure: Richards himself laid the double brick walls.[7] By early February 1911 the house was completed and the Rutherford family of four moved in (Hazel a day later than the others: until she recovered from a bout with typhoid, Hazel stayed with Mrs. Bob Douglas).

Until early 1909 the university area was still farm and bush land on the western outskirts of Strathcona. By the end of 1909, however, the foundation for the arts building was nearing completion, and nearby excavations marked the future residences of Dr. Rutherford, Dr. H. M. Tory, Dr. D. G. Revell, and Walter K. Pierce of the government telephone system. Construction of these houses followed in 1910. A photograph[8] taken that year shows the Rutherford house nearing completion, and the more modest Pierce house already constructed immediately to the south; an old log barn, a vestige of the Simpson farm on river lot five, stood northwest of Rutherford House.[9]

The Rutherford grounds were attractively landscaped with a terrace and a low stone wall that still surrounds the front half of the house. The wall, two and one-half feet high (three-quarters of a metre), built with rocks from the Rutherford property on Mill Creek,[10] is breached at the front and west side by stone steps. The front steps were originally approached from Saskatchewan Avenue by a circular driveway or carriage sweep that enclosed a flower garden and a grove of trees.[11] A brick garage to house Rutherford's large red Packard was built immediately southeast of the house and featured a grease pit and a gasoline storage tank.[12] The garage was approached by a crooked driveway from 112 Street. Rutherford hired a local gardener to landscape the grounds with trees and bushes, and to erect a little rustic summer house close to the intersection of 112 Street and Saskatchewan Avenue.[13] The summer house was used not only by the Rutherfords, but by many courting students as well.[14]

Both Dr. and Mrs. Rutherford were ardent gardeners. He spent many hours each year either tending a large vegetable garden or planting and tending additional trees, hedge, and lilacs.[15] Mrs. Rutherford enjoyed her flower gardens and always decorated the house with blooms before she received guests. Rutherford's reverence for trees is illustrated by the fact that he would not have a Christmas tree in the house: rather, a large Christmas cactus was moved from the living room to the dining room during the festive season.[16]

Completed at a cost of $25,000,[17] the new house was one of the finest constructed in Edmonton prior to World War I. Generous in scale, it encompassed over 4,000 square feet (370 square metres) of living space on the two main floors alone. Unlike most Edmonton homes of the era, it incorporated a guest room, a breakfast room, a library, den, and maid's quarters, in addition to the normal functional spaces such as kitchen and dining room. And with such features as central hot water heating, electric lighting, running water, flush toilets, built-in closets, skylights, and a telephone, the house was ultramodern for 1911.

Stylistically, the house combined Elizabethan and Jacobean motifs in a then-fashionable style often termed "Jacobethan." The exterior use of red brick with sandstone trim, tall chimneys, Doric-columned porches, and two-storey bay windows all exemplify this style. Rutherford's house would have graced any fashionable neighborhood in Toronto or Chicago of the time; in 1911 Edmonton it was a home worthy of a premier.

The interior confirms that this was a house designed for both residence and reception. The rooms are arranged around a grand central hall and staircase lavishly detailed in oak. Ceilings are 11 feet (3.4 metres) high and the main rooms are spaciously proportioned. The dining room, the largest room in the house excluding the attic, contains 350 square feet (32.5 square metres) and features a bay window 12 feet wide (3.7 metres), with fir wainscotting and decorative fir ceiling beams. Next in size, the parlour contains 300 square feet (28 square metres) and a similar bay window. The library, 240 square feet (22 square metres) in area, has fir bookshelves from floor to ceiling, a handsome brick fireplace,[18] and sliding panel doors opening into the dining room. A second wood and coal-burning fireplace[19] is located in the den,[20] a cosy 13-by-14-foot (4-by-4.3 metre) room that presents a wide, arched entrance to the 10-by-13-foot (3-by-4 metre) breakfast room. The 350-square-foot (32.5-square-metre) kitchen area is divided into a cooking area, two side-by-side pantries, a serving and access area, and a service stairway leading up to the maid's quarters and down to the basement.

The front entrance hall, stairway landing, and upper hall are given particular warmth and beauty by the generous use of oak panelling and a stained glass skylight above the landing. There is extensive use of oak throughout the central core of the house, on the grand staircase, the balustrades, the newell posts, and the pediments above the lower hall doorways. The four second-storey bedrooms open onto the most spacious area of the house, a vast 500-square-foot (47-square-metre) hall, ornamented by an oak balustrade around the stairwell. A similar balustrade defines the front area of the hall that was used as a sewing and sitting room. Three of the bedrooms each exceed 250 square feet (23 square metres) in area, while the fourth bedroom and the maid's quarters are more modestly proportioned.

Although the original attic had no windows, it was lit by three skylights. Two dormer windows were installed when the house became a fraternity residence in the 1940s. Apparently there was originally no protective barrier around the stained glass skylight set in the attic floor.

The front area of the basement, separated from the rest of the basement by a brick partition where steel posts now stand, was initially an unfinished dugout used for vegetable storage.[21] Hot water radiators heated the house. The boiler, originally fired with coal, was replaced by gas burners in the 1920s. Part of the basement was used as a laundry room, an arrangement that relieved the kitchen of that function.

Figure 54: Rutherford House and garage from the southwest, c. 1914.
(Mrs. Hazel McCuaig)

Figure 55: Rutherford House and summer house from 112 Street, c. 1914.
(Mrs. Hazel McCuaig)

Interior spaces were either public or private in character. The public areas, normally accessible to guests, included the upper and lower halls and connecting main staircase, the parlour, library, and dining room. The rest of the house, with the partial exception of the northeast guest bedroom, was the private domain of the Rutherford family and their intimates. Maple flooring is found throughout the public areas; the flooring in the private areas is fir. Another double standard exists with respect to doorway dimensions: public doorways are high and wide, while the others are lower and narrower. Similarly, unlike the grand stairway inside the front door, all three stairways at the back of the house are steep and narrow. Several concessions in the quality of the building materials were discovered during the restoration of the house. For example, the plaster downstairs proved to be much harder and more durable than the plaster upstairs.[22]

The kitchen area was both a crossroads and a private area of the house. Its complex and inefficient layout betrays the transitional position it occupies between traditional and modern domestic food-preparation areas. Equipped with electric lights, hot water radiators, hot and cold running water, an ice box in the adjoining porch, and a kitchen cupboard, it was a far cry from the incoherent, cluttered, and labour-intensive domestic work areas of the nineteenth century. Yet by later standards its components were scattered and dysfunctional. The preparation of a meal might well have required trips to the ice box in the back porch, to the east food-storage pantry, to the basement for vegetables, to the kitchen table (which blocked the doorway to the hall), and to the stove and sink. Serving added trips to the dining room or breakfast room. Besides the great carrying distances involved, this procedure required that Mrs. Rutherford or the maid open and close several doors and negotiate a flight of stairs. The design of the kitchen area alone virtually presupposed one or even two maids.

The Rutherfords moved into this new house with the furnishings of their much smaller home, and apart from new dining room and library furniture, they added little to what they already possessed.[23] The new Rutherford house consequently appeared to be sparsely furnished, a condition that preserved its interior spaciousness and easily permitted large groups to gather within its walls. The house was assigned the address 11153 Saskatchewan Avenue, but Dr. Rutherford named it "Achnacarry" after the ancestral castle of the Camerons in the County of Inverness, Scotland.[24]

When the house was first occupied in 1911, Dr. and Mrs. Rutherford used the master bedroom on the northwest corner, while Cecil took the smaller bedroom behind it and Hazel the one opposite Cecil's. The northeast bedroom, equipped with a small bathroom, was reserved for guests. Visitors were received in the front hall, the parlour, or the library. The large attic, approximately 900 square feet (84 square metres) exclusive of the eaves, was used for trunks and general storage and for drying clothes in the winter. Mrs. McCuaig remembers that the many designs submitted for Alberta's coat of arms were ranged around the attic for several weeks.

In 1915–16, motivated by wartime patriotism, Hazel trained as a nurse for a year at Wellesley Hospital in Toronto, but she returned to Rutherford House in 1916 just as

Figure 56: Aerial view of the University of Alberta, 1929.
Rutherford House in right foreground.
(University of Alberta Archives, 69-10-29)

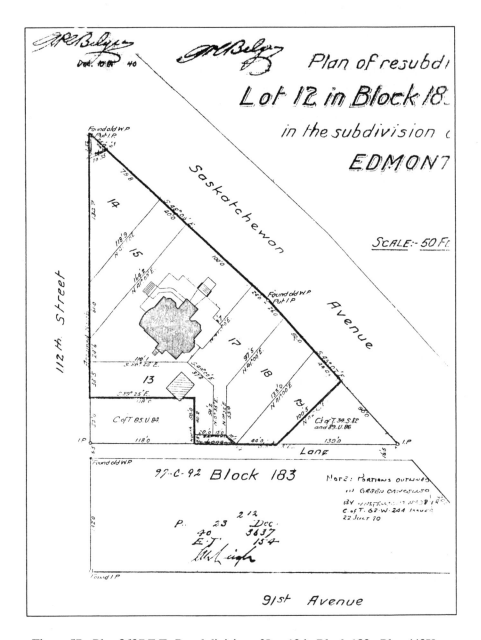

Figure 57: Plan 3637 E.T., Resubdivision of Lot 12 in Block 183 - Plan 443X,
1928, Rutherford House superimposed.
(Land Titles Office, Edmonton)

Cecil prepared to go overseas. On 5 June 1916 Helen Reid Martin, daughter of one of Strathcona's pioneer families, had become Cecil's bride. Later that year the groom went overseas and served with the British Royal Garrison Artillery for the balance of World War I.[25] Helen occupied his room in Rutherford House from 1916 to 1919. Upon Cecil's return to Edmonton the couple moved into their own home. On 17 September 1919 Hazel Rutherford married Stanley Harwood McCuaig,[26] the young lawyer who had articled with her father's law firm. After a few months in their own home the McCuaigs returned to live in Rutherford House from 1920 to 1924, occupying the west side of the house (the den, breakfast room, and two west bedrooms).[27] Dr. and Mrs. Rutherford used the east side. During this period three children were born to the McCuaigs: Eric in 1920, Ruth in 1922, and Helen in 1924. Eric was born in the master bedroom.[28] In 1924 the McCuaigs moved into their new house at 9117 - 112 Street on the original lot twelve, immediately southwest of Rutherford House.[29] For the next sixteen years Dr. and Mrs. Rutherford, together with a maid or housekeeper,[30] occupied their big house alone, except for the school term 1938–39 when Eric McCuaig again resided at Achnacarry. However, there was an endless stream of visitors, not to mention four lively grandchildren from next door, Harwood McCuaig having been born in 1926.[31]

In 1928 Dr. Rutherford had lot twelve subdivided into nine smaller lots, one of which was already occupied by the McCuaigs: this lot was enlarged from 50 by 91 feet (15 by 28 metres) to 50 by 118 feet (15 by 36 metres). Rutherford House still occupied the largest lot. With 100 feet (30.5 metres) of frontage on Saskatchewan Avenue, it contained almost a third of an acre (eight of an hectare).[32]

On 13 September 1940, following a lengthy illness, Mrs. Rutherford died in the house.[33] Soon afterwards Dr. Rutherford went to live with Cecil and Helen Rutherford, where he stayed until his death on 11 June 1941. Late in 1940 Rutherford sold the lot, the house, and most of its furnishings.[34]

Although the house was never the premier's residence it was originally intended to be, it nevertheless fulfilled its purpose in many other ways: it was the setting for hundreds of important events in the social life of Strathcona and Edmonton for a period of almost thirty years. Moreover, because of its location and Rutherford's intimate association with the university, the house was long an integral part of the university campus.

Perhaps the first social event to occur in the house was a small afternoon tea given by Mrs. Rutherford on 2 September 1911, when about twenty guests were invited to meet distinguished visitors from Toronto. Mrs. Rutherford received her guests in the library, which was decorated with asters. Tea was served in a dining room adorned with pink sweet peas, while a small orchestra played in the parlour.[35] Another afternoon tea given by Mrs. Rutherford two months later was described as "an important social event" that attracted "hundreds of ladies" from both sides of the river despite a chilling drizzle. A young neighbour, Master Revell, opened the door for the guests, and Mrs. Rutherford received them in the parlour. The *Strathcona Plaindealer* went on to note that

> the spacious rooms with their many flowers and lights, music and warmth, were even more than usually attractive in contrast to the drizzling rain and dull skies of the outside world. And the gracious personality of the hostess gave all that was wanted to complete the charm, as she greeted her guests... wearing a handsome dress of cream crepe de chene embroidered with pearls .... The tea table was very pretty and inviting with its large bowl of red roses, red candles in cut glass candle sticks, rich lace centre piece and doyley.... Miss Hazel Rutherford, the young daughter of the house, in a pretty embroidered frock of white, with a number of Varsity girl friends, helped in passing refreshments. From the music room came sounds of sweet music as Turner's orchestra gave selections throughout the afternoon. The library, with its books and big bright fire attracted many guests....[36]

Three weeks later Mrs. Rutherford gave yet another tea that attracted "a very large number of callers,"[37] and in April 1912 she gave a luncheon in honour of Mrs. C. A. Stuart, the wife of the university's chancellor.[38] On 5 July 1912 she gave a special tea for the ladies of the Baptist church on the occasion of the departure of one of their active members, who received a silver tea service.[39]

On the evening of 29 January 1912 Rutherford House was the scene of a musicale sponsored by the Keomi Chapter of the I.O.D.E., of which Mrs. Rutherford was a member. The evening had been organized to raise money for the proposed university hospital. Dr. and Mrs. Rutherford welcomed the arrivals, who paid an admission of fifty cents to hear a varied programme of instrumental and vocal pieces and readings by local artists:

> The beautiful and spacious rooms were filled with well-known people from both sides of the river. ... After the programme refreshments were served and a pleasant social time succeeded. As a result of the musicale a good sum was realized.[40]

On 9 May 1912 an event occurred at Rutherford House that initiated what was to become a traditional part of the university's graduation activities:

> Yesterday afternoon the members of the graduating class of the University were most pleasantly entertained by Dr. and Mrs. Rutherford at their home near the University. Yesterday was Founder's Day, and as Dr. Rutherford is universally esteemed the founder of the University of Alberta, a tour of the University grounds on the annual pilgrimage could not be regarded as complete without special reference to Dr. and Mrs. Rutherford. Dainty refreshments were served from the prettiest tea-table, artistically finished in

the University colours, green and gold, with green candles. An anniversary cake, with four candles, two in yellow and two in green indicated the 4th anniversary day.[41]

The Founder's Day Tea for graduands was an annual event at Rutherford House for the next twenty-six years. From the twenty-five students who attended in 1912, the numbers swelled to three hundred in 1938,[42] yet Mrs. Rutherford continued to personally make the necessary preparations, for it was an event she genuinely enjoyed. During those years she missed only one tea, when she was visiting a sister who was ill in Ottawa.[43] Dr. Rutherford too missed only one tea, in 1927 when he was absent in the East.[44] On 9 May 1938, during what was to be the final Founder's Day Tea, he proudly although mistakenly observed that he had been host to every graduating class in the history of the university.[45]

Just before the tea at Rutherford House each year, the graduating class planted a tree on the campus; Mrs. McCuaig remembers watching the tree-planting from an upstairs window and counting the members of the group so that her mother would know how many were coming for tea. Dr. Rutherford always welcomed the graduating class and congratulated them on their success. At the 1935 tea he encouraged them to face the world with confidence and determination despite the crisis in employment during those depression years.[46] At the Founder's Day Tea in 1931, Dr. and Mrs. Rutherford were privileged to have Lieutenant-Governor and Mrs. Walsh assist them in receiving the graduands.[47] From 1928 to 1938 Dr. Rutherford, by then chancellor of the University of Alberta, conferred degrees on the same students that he had entertained at tea only a day or two before. L. G. Thomas, one of the many university graduates who attended the tea at Rutherford House, remembers that the "annual Founder's Day tea party was a gracious and refreshingly personal aspect of the ceremonies attending the annual graduation exercises."[48]

Students and faculty members of the university were among the most frequent visitors to Rutherford House for the thirty years Dr. Rutherford lived there; his house and library were virtually an extension of the university. Professor Morden Long finally prevailed on Rutherford to institute a sign-out book to better ensure the safety of his collection of rare books. Rutherford was extremely well-read in Canadian history, and he communicated his enthusiasm for the subject to many students during innumerable chats with them in his library. In a letter to his father in 1920, Professor P. A. W. Wallace, then newly appointed to the English Department at the University of Alberta, spoke of his first visit to Rutherford House:

Ex-premier Rutherford has the best collection of Canadiana in Alberta. Broadus gave me an introduction to him, and I had an interesting evening in his library. He told me with pride that one branch of his family came to Ontario in 1834. Whereupon I told him that my great grandfather came to Ontario in 1826. He was impressed.[49]

Professor E. K. Broadus, head of the English Department and one of the four original faculty members of the university, was a close friend and frequent visitor at Rutherford House. He fondly referred to the small cheese sandwiches that Mrs. Rutherford served as "bird's nests."[50] Donalda Dickie spent many hours in Rutherford's library researching material for her history books for young people.[51] Other prominent visitors to the house included Cyrus Eaton, Lieutenant-Governor J. C. Bowen, Bob Edwards, the editor of the *Calgary Eye Opener*, and J. Hamilton McDonald, former editor of the *Strathcona Plaindealer*. One unwelcome visitor to the house in the 1930s was a nocturnal caller wearing running shoes. The thief gained access to the building through a window in the breakfast room and made away with Rutherford's watch that lay on a night table beside its sleeping owner. Mrs. Rutherford subsequently resorted to laying a plank between the front and inner doors of the vestibule to foil future intruders.[52]

Rutherford's wide circle of friends and associates in the many organizations in which he was active also shared in the legendary hospitality at Rutherford House. As president of the Historical Society of Alberta, Rutherford often hosted the society meetings at his home, and "those members who attended will never forget the warm welcome they received on these occasions from their genial host and hostess."[53] Similarly, members of the Canadian Authors' Association, the Y.W.C.A. advisory board, the St. Andrew's Society, the Strathcona Baptist Church, and the McGill University Alumni Association fondly remember the meetings they attended in the big dining room at Rutherford House. Mrs. Rutherford also hosted numerous meetings of the organizations to which she belonged: the Women's Canadian Club, the Women's University Club, the Imperial Order Daughters of the Empire (Keomi Chapter), the Women's Missionary Society of Metropolitan United Church, Strathcona Baptist Church, and the Granite Ladies' Curling Club.[54]

Two particularly notable occasions in the history of the house were the wedding of Hazel Rutherford in 1919 and the golden wedding anniversary of Dr. and Mrs. Rutherford in 1938. Hazel Rutherford and Stanley McCuaig were married in the living room of Rutherford House on the morning of Wednesday, 17 September 1919:

Rev. (Capt.) J. C. Bowen performed the ceremony in the presence of only a few intimate friends and relatives of the bride and groom. The home was particularly attractively decorated with autumn leaves, sweet peas and roses. Mr. and Mrs. McCuaig left on the noon train for a honeymoon trip to Lagan [Lake Louise], and on their return will live on 80th ave.[55]

The golden wedding anniversary of Dr. and Mrs. Rutherford on 19 December 1938 represented a climax in their long lives and in the history of Rutherford House. Some two hundred invited guests attended the celebration and reception to pay tribute to two of Alberta's outstanding pioneers. The guests represented a large section of Alberta's institutional life: the government, university, business, church, legal, civic, and social circles in which the Rutherfords moved. Some of the most notable guests were Premier

William Aberhart; Dr. W. A. R. Kerr, president of the University of Alberta; Col. F. C. Jamieson, Rutherford's former partner in law; Dr. Donalda Dickie; Lieutenant- Governor J. C. Bowen; Mayor J. W. Fry; and the Hon. Mr. Justice W. R. Howson. A pleasantly unexpected guest for Dr. Rutherford was Pipe Major Arthur Miller, invited by Stanley McCuaig as a surprise for his father-in-law. Miller piped up and down the grand staircase and around the upstairs hallway, filling the house with sounds dear to Rutherford's heart.[56] The *Edmonton Bulletin* described the occasion in colourful detail:

> Masses of gold chrysanthemums, bronze and mauve baby 'mums were used in profusion throughout the spacious rooms . . . for the occasion, while in the reception room where Dr. and Mrs. Rutherford received, a huge bouquet of huge yellow roses, [a] gift from the class of 1912, the first graduating class of the University of Alberta was a lovely background. A bouquet of huge yellow gold chrysanthemums, gift from the McGill Alumni Association, was placed in the hall. . . . Tea was served from a table simply yet beautifully laid in white lace, and centred with a low bowl of yellow rosebuds, a gift from the family. Tapers in gold flanked the bowl of flowers and a three-tiered wedding cake was placed on an adjoining buffet. Pastel tinted tapers were placed on either side. A birthday cake for Master Harwood McCuaig whose twelfth birthday occurs on Tuesday, was placed on a separate table.[57]

The *Edmonton Journal* also covered the event:

> Giving further expression to the felicitations which had been extended to them all day in letters, telegrams and floral tributes, Dr. and Mrs. Rutherford were made the recipients Monday night of gifts from guests who had come to honour them. Hon. J. C. Bowen, the Lieutenant-Governor, made the presentation of a purse of gold to Dr. Rutherford, and Mrs. Bowen gave Mrs. Rutherford a bouquet of roses.[58]

Neither Dr. nor Mrs. Rutherford would reveal their ages: "We're still young enough to have a good time anyway," laughed Dr. Rutherford as he chatted with his guests.[59]

When there were no guests to be entertained, Dr. Rutherford was usually in the library reading, or perusing new book catalogues for acquisitions to his library. Buying books was a temptation he was unable to resist. Because Mrs. Rutherford occasionally tried to curb this appetite, he sometimes brought new books into the house concealed on his person and immediately put them on the bookshelves in the hope that she would not notice.[60] Rutherford usually sat at a table to the right of the fireplace where he could spread out his books and papers. If he had a speech to give he did not write it out, but merely listed headings and spoke spontaneously.[61] From spring to fall he spent many hours in the vegetable garden or tending the grounds, activities that gave him the opportunity to talk with neighbours. Rutherford's grandson, Eric McCuaig, recalls

Figure 58: Dr. and Mrs. Rutherford in their library on their golden wedding anniversary, 19 December 1938.
(Mrs. Hazel McCuaig)

Figure 59: Family gathering on the Rutherfords' golden wedding anniversary, 19 December 1938. Back row, left to right: Stanley H., Ruth, and Eric McCuaig, Mattie Rutherford; Hazel McCuaig; Dr. A.C. and Cecil Rutherford. Front row, left to right: Harwood McCuaig, Helen and Margaret Rutherford; Helen McCuaig. (Mrs. Hazel McCuaig)

that during the 1920s and 1930s his grandfather provided small garden plots and expert gardening advice for several children in the neighbourhood, including Eric himself. Fall evenings would often find him standing by a bonfire of raked leaves chatting with neighbourhood friends.[62]

Mrs. Rutherford was an excellent cook and housekeeper who took great pride in her home. Skilled at sewing, knitting, and embroidery, she took prizes for her point lace and knitting at some of the early Strathcona summer fairs.[63] From time to time a seamstress would visit the house and, guided by Mrs. Rutherford, make clothing for the family in the upstairs sewing room. Many of Mrs. Rutherford's leisure hours were spent at the keyboard of the Nordheimer upright piano playing her favourite hymns and gospel songs. If there was wallpapering to be done, it was Mrs. Rutherford who climbed the ladder and Dr. Rutherford who held it. Occasionally the family played croquet out on the lawn or viewed distant parts of the world through their stereopticon. Mrs. Rutherford looked after the family pets, two British bulldogs named Jellicoe and Patsy, a black spaniel named Bunty, and a black Pomeranian named Belgium.[64] When there was no maid to occupy the rear suite, the Rutherfords made use of the maid's sitting room overlooking the campus. The overflow of books and pamphlets from Dr. Rutherford's library was also kept there.

Mrs. McCuaig remembers her mother as a quiet, shy woman. Very much an Edwardian lady, she was wary of drunks and Indians and frightened of such things as thunderstorms and horses. The pet bulldogs, Jellicoe and Patsy, were kept for protection and they gave Mrs. Rutherford a much-needed sense of security. Her warm hospitality was legendary. At her funeral at Strathcona Baptist Church on 16 September 1940, Dr. G. A. MacDonald spoke of the kindness, generosity, and aid she had extended to so many university students now scattered throughout the world: "She made her home a haven of loving devotion, and one of the bulwarks of western civilization. It has always remained so."[65]

Shortly after Mrs. Rutherford's death on 13 September 1940, Dr. Rutherford moved out of his house. By the end of the year he had arranged the sale of the home to the Delta Upsilon Fraternity for $9,500. This price included the house, most of the furnishings, and the lot, but not the library contents or the brick garage.[66] Members of the family removed some of the furnishings before the transaction. In 1940–41 university staff went through Rutherford's library and selected a large number of volumes for the university collection. The balance of the books was divided between Cecil Rutherford and Hazel McCuaig. Most of these were also acquired by the university in 1950.

Late in 1940 Delta Upsilon member Ed Bate moved into Rutherford House as caretaker (he would later marry Rutherford's granddaughter, Ruth McCuaig), and in 1941 the other members of the fraternity occupied the house. It remained the Delta Upsilon residence until 1969. The fraternity population in the house varied from twenty to twenty-five students each year and, though the house was used much more intensively than formerly, it withstood the wear extremely well. Some well-known political figures, including former premier Peter Lougheed and members of his cabinet, lived in Rutherford House as Delta Upsilon members. Commenting on how well the house had survived as a fraternity residence, Dr. Allan Warrack, minister of utilities (1975 –79) in the Lougheed government, noted that "people really respected the house because of its history. That was one of the advantages of living here."[67]

By 1961 the University of Alberta was planning to expand eastward across 112 Street between Saskatchewan Drive and 87 Avenue. This fine residential area, which included Rutherford House, was scheduled for demolition in the late sixties to provide space for such needed facilities as student housing, a humanities centre, and a law building. On 25 February 1966 the university, in conjunction with the Department of Public Works, gave notice to all residents of North Garneau between 88 Avenue and Saskatchewan Drive and between 111 and 112 Streets that they would require possession of these properties by 1 May 1967 to carry out the expansion programme.[68] Stanley McCuaig immediately sent letters to the president of the university, Dr. Walter Johns, and to the mayor of Edmonton, V. M. Dantzer, outlining the contributions of Dr. Rutherford to the university and the city and urging the preservation of Rutherford House in recognition of these contributions.[69] On 3 May 1966 professor of history L. G. Thomas submitted a proposal to the chairman of the university's academic planning committee to preserve and restore Rutherford House.[70]

By late 1966, however, the university board of governors had decided that the historic home must be demolished. According to Dr. B. E. Riedel, chairman of the campus planning committee,

> the city, province and other bodies have considered this matter, and the board of governors has decided that expansion of the university is more important. A commemorative plaque, preserving "the idea" of the home, would be erected at the site when the new building is put up.[71]

The imminent destruction of yet another historic landmark in Edmonton soon became a public issue. In November 1966 Mrs. Lila Fahlman, a resident of North Garneau, and a number of concerned people organized the Society for the Preservation of Historic Homes.[72] Under Mrs. Fahlman's leadership, the society launched what would become a four-year campaign of briefs, letters, petitions, and publicity to save Rutherford House. In May 1967 the university announced that the scheduled demolition of the house would be postponed for one year, until May 1968. In April 1968 the university purchased the building from Delta Upsilon Fraternity but granted permission to the fraternity to remain in the house until May 1969.[73]

In 1969 a ten-year development study of the university's growth recommended that almost all of the existing buildings on campus be retained. A. J. Diamond, an architect involved in the study, commented that the old buildings were part of the university's character and could be adapted to future plans and needs. "We would like to save [Rutherford House]; there is no need to destroy it," he said.[74]

By this time numerous other organizations had entered the campaign to save the house, including the University Women's Club, the Women's Canadian Club, the Northern Alberta Pioneers and Old Timers Association, the Historical Society of Alberta, the Edmonton Historical Board, the Human History Division of the Provincial Museum, and the City of Edmonton. The University Women's Club, for example, asked the board of governors to turn Rutherford House over to them as a club headquarters on the condition that they restore the house to its original condition.[75] In June 1969 the university announced that demolition of Rutherford House would be delayed for yet another year and that a special meeting would be held with groups working to save the building. At this meeting, held on 10 October 1969, the Board building committee reiterated its previous recommendation that the building be demolished. It cited the high cost of renovation, the present state of the house and its surroundings, the fact that Rutherford's first house was to be preserved, and the siting needs of the planned humanities complex, which was scheduled to be under construction by April 1970.[76]

The University Women's Club, through its Rutherford House study group convened by Mrs. Rita Calhoun, immediately intensified its campaign to preserve and restore the building. The club explored the possibility of withdrawing its $14,000 investment in the university scholarship fund to add to the $12,000 fund it had already raised to restore Rutherford House. (Estimates of the cost of restoration varied from $30,000 to $250,000 depending on several factors, including which side of the dispute the estimate supported.)[77] Basing their case on a renovation estimate of $35–40,000 and the funds they had raised, the University Women's Club made a final plea to the board of governors and Premier Harry Strom in early December 1969 to spare the house. The board of governors made no commitment, but the provincial government promised to study the proposal.

In December 1969 a committee of three ministers (Ambrose Hollowach, Bob Clark, and A. W. Ludwig) was formed to investigate the possibility of preserving and restoring the site. The committee requested an evaluation of the house by the Provincial Museum and Archives, and a report was prepared during January 1970 by historic sites officer John Nicks. The report[78] gave highest recommendation to the complete restoration and furnishing of Rutherford House as a historic house museum on the grounds of its historical and architectural value. It further recommended that the university be asked to reconsider its development plan for the North Garneau area, making provision for adaptive use of the home. A cost and feasibility study was subsequently prepared by Department of Public Works architect Bob Anderson, who found the building structurally sound for renovation at an estimated cost of $70,000.[79]

In October 1970 Minister of Public Works A. W. Ludwig announced that Rutherford House was to be preserved. The university board of governors then revealed their decision to lease the house to the Department of Public Works for forty years at one dollar per year on condition that the exterior of the house be renovated by 1 June 1972 and the building be used as a museum or historic site. The Department of Public Works allocated $50,000 for renovations to the house for the spring of 1971.[80] Meanwhile, the house sat empty over the winter of 1970–71. Vandals broke into the unguarded building and stripped it of many of its decorative features, smashed the stained glass skylight, and tore the thermostat off the wall. Water pipes and radiators froze and burst, and the resulting water damage increased the eventual cost of restoration by another $50,000.[81]

In the fall of 1971 a Department of Public Works crew, under the direction of architect Bob Anderson and construction manager Doug Laine, began the restoration of Rutherford House.[82] Lacking precise guidelines on how the building was to be used following restoration, Anderson had it classified under "building classification group A, division 2: assembly occupancies." This includes, for example, art galleries, museums, non-residential clubs, and exhibition and lecture halls. Thus, as well as functioning as a museum or place of historical interest, the house could accommodate up to fifty people for meetings, teas, or lectures. To meet the code requirements of this classification, certain upgrading measures were needed. The floor assemblies immediately above the basement were brought to three-quarter-hour fire separation, and the combustible roof assemblies were brought to a three-quarter-hour fire resistance rating. In addition, the electrical system was completely rewired and three water closets were installed.

The task of restoring the house consisted essentially of removing alien features installed during Delta Upsilon's occupancy, and of repairing damaged or deteriorated elements in the house. No attempt was made to restore the basement, the kitchen, the maid's quarters, any of the washrooms, or the attic to an original condition. Besides the evidence provided by careful stripping of the interior finishing, valuable information about the original appearance of the house was provided by Mrs. Hazel McCuaig, who also furnished a number of early photographs. The exterior was restored during the fall of 1971, and in June of 1972 the interior work was completed. The cost of restoration was $120,000 plus the cost of installing water, gas, electricity, and telephone services. As per the agreement with the university board of governors, all restoration and subsequent maintenance and utility costs were borne by the provincial government.

The restoration process had to remedy the twin problems of removing room partitions and other structural changes made by the fraternity, and repairing or replacing original fabric damaged over the years. On the outside of the house, the Delta Upsilon interlocking shingle roofing and the original cedar shingle roofing beneath were removed and replaced with cedar shingles dipped in black penetrating stain. Flashing and bitumen roofing were applied to the gutters and the three skylights were replaced. The deteriorated brick coping on the parapets was repaired using original bricks from the back porch, which had sagged and separated from the house. The back porch was completely dismantled and rebuilt with new bricks. The

Figure 60: Delta Upsilon Fraternity House (1940–1969), c. 1969.
(Alberta Government Photo)

Figure 61: Restoration architect Bob Anderson at the rear entrance of Rutherford House, October 1971.
(Alberta Government Photo)

Figure 62: Department of Public Works restoration crew in the kitchen of Rutherford House, October 1971.
(Alberta Government Photo)

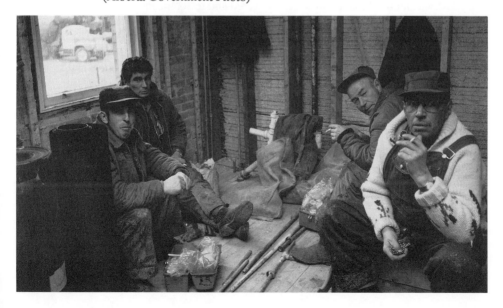

substructure and floor of the sun porch were also replaced with new material, as were rotted mullions and muntins, which were reglazed in a few places. The balcony floor had rotted extensively and was repaired and reroofed; the balustrade on the balcony was extensively repaired. The plinths under the front columns were replaced and the columns repaired. All exterior wood was sanded and repainted. The brick walls were in good condition and required very little repointing, a tribute to the fine original workmanship.

Work in the basement was essentially a clean-up operation: removal of Delta Upsilon furnishings such as the bar, cubicles, showers, and a washroom (the imitation fireplace, wooden flooring, wash-tubs, and the steel posts and beam were retained). Code requirements were met by applying gypsum board to the ceiling for adequate fire separation. The main basement stairway was rebuilt and the boiler relined. A new gas line was installed and black iron piping replaced leaking, corroded, and damaged pipes in the heating distribution system.

On the main floor, all rooms were restored except the kitchen area. The tile floor and underlay in the main hall were removed and replaced with new maple flooring that closely matched the sanded and refinished flooring in the adjoining rooms. The kitchen, den, breakfast room, and parlour were replastered, and the ceiling in the library and dining room was replaced; this made it possible to replace joists and studding showing dry rot, and to install insulation and a vapour barrier wherever the strapping was exposed on outside walls. Both fireplaces were repaired, with particular attention paid to the den fireplace where the cracked and crazed tile was completely replaced and the inglenook was rebuilt. Another stained glass window from the chapel at the old Misericordia Hospital was installed in the vestibule. The two doorways between the kitchen and breakfast room were uncovered and restored, and the breakfast room arch was re-opened. New linoleum was laid in the kitchen and pantry. Only one decorative pediment and half a newell post head had survived, and from these models new ones were fabricated and installed. The wedges and mortices in the main stairway were tightened and missing balusters were replaced. Oak surfaces (panels and stairway) were patched and refinished.

All areas on the second floor were restored except the maid's quarters (reserved for office and storage space) and the washrooms, which were renovated for visitor use.[83] Secondary panelling and acoustic tile and the old plaster behind it were removed and replaced with new plaster, while resilient tile and underlay were removed from original flooring, which was repaired, sanded, and refinished. The partition between the sewing room and the hall was removed and replaced by a balustrade. Ceiling areas exposed to cold attic spaces were insulated. A new stained glass skylight was constructed by Winter Art Glass Studio of Edmonton and doors salvaged from the demolished Edmonton courthouse were installed in the bedrooms. All discarded molding, trim, coving, and baseboard was replaced. The partitioned closet in the guest room was re-opened, and a partition was installed to replace the sliding doors of the closet in the master bedroom. The window in the stairway leading to the attic was

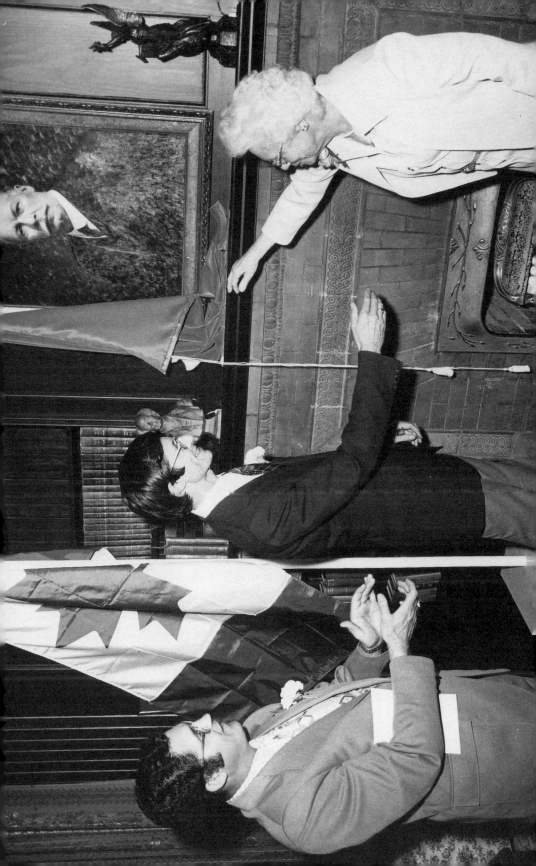

Figure 63: Official opening of Rutherford House, 11 May 1974. Left to right:
Hon. Dr. Allan Warrack, Hon. Lou Hyndman, Mrs. Hazel McCuaig.
(Alberta Government Photo)

Figure 64: Rutherford House restored, 1974.
(Historic Sites Service)

Figure 65: The library in Rutherford House, n.d.
(Mrs. Hazel McCuaig)

restored, replacing the door installed by the fraternity. In the attic, cracked and crumbling plaster was removed, the rafters were insulated, and the area was replastered. The two dormer windows installed by the fraternity were retained. A new safety barrier was erected around the stained glass skylight. Radiators salvaged from several government buildings around the province replaced those damaged by freezing, and suitable fixtures were found in antique shops or at auctions. Telephone outlets were installed on the first and second floors, and a conduit for an automatic fire detection system was also installed.

On 6 June 1972, as the restoration project neared completion, a meeting of personnel from the Department of Public Works and the Provincial Museum and Archives of Alberta was held at Rutherford House to assess the project and to consider potential adaptive uses of the building:

It was generally agreed by the PMAA staff present that the restoration work carried out by DPW is of high quality.

.... Repair of the exterior and interior was meticulously executed. Perhaps most notable of all was the excellent reconstruction of missing portions of decorative woodwork in the interior.[84]

Figure 66: The Library of
Rutherford House
after restoration.

Bob Anderson today pays tribute to the quality of workmanship given by the public works crew and by Doug Laine, the project's construction foreman.[85]

Research and acquisition of suitable furnishings, some of them original to the house, were carried out in 1972 and 1973 by the Provincial Museum. On 10 June 1973 the restored and partially refurnished house museum was opened to the public.[86] The official opening of the house took place on 11 May 1974 and was attended by Mrs. Hazel McCuaig and several representatives of the provincial government and the University of Alberta.[87]

Mrs. McCuaig unveiled the photographic copy of William Everitt's portrait of her father that now hangs over the fireplace in the library. In a way, Dr. Rutherford had come home again to Achnacarry.

$*$ $*$ $*$

Work continues on the restoration, furnishing, and interpretation of Rutherford House, now the responsibilities of the Historic Sites Service of Alberta Culture and Multiculturalism. In 1983 the kitchen area was restored and furnished to its 1915 appearance, and the opening of this part of the house to visitors has provided excellent opportunities for the interpretive staff. The interpretation programme has broadened

Figure 67: The dining room in Rutherford House, 17 September 1919. The table
is decorated for Hazel Rutherford's wedding.
(Mrs. Hazel McCuaig)

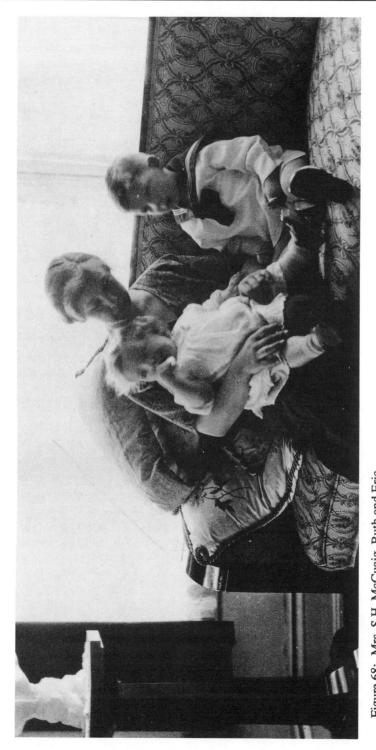

Figure 68: Mrs. S.H. McCuaig, Ruth and Eric McCuaig in the parlour of Rutherford House, c. 1923. (Mrs. Hazel McCuaig)

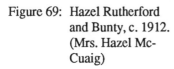

Figure 69: Hazel Rutherford and Bunty, c. 1912. (Mrs. Hazel Mc-Cuaig)

Figure 70: Cecil Rutherford and Jellicoe, c. 1920. (Mrs. Helen Rutherford)

Figure 71: The Rutherford gravestone, Mount Pleasant Cemetery.
(Historic Sites Service, 79R267-7)

greatly since the opening of this historic site, designated a Provincial Historic Resource on 28 June 1979. Though much remains to be done, visitors today are able to enjoy group or single tours of most of the house, and participate in special events and theme tours, as well as musical performances, craft demonstrations, and historical dramas. During 1988 the lower level of the house was finished with a modern kitchen, laundry,and boardroom, offices and public washrooms. In a joint project, the Delta Upsilon Fraternity Alumni and the Friends of Rutherford House, finished the boardroom in oak panelling and installed oak furniture for what was named the Delta Upsilon Visitors' Centre. On the main floor, the Friends of Rutherford House opened a seasonal tea room and gift shop in the den and sun porch. As it was during Rutherford's residence there, Achnacarry continues to be a vital and welcoming social institution in the community, and—as Rutherford would have wished—still a part of the university landscape.

EPILOGUE

In 1960 when A. D. Marzolf began work on his M.Ed. thesis entitled "Alexander Cameron Rutherford and his Influence on Alberta's Educational Program," he was surprised by the relative obscurity of the man who had formed Alberta's first government and played such an important role in Alberta education. He found it strange

that no major work has been written on a man of such importance to the province of Alberta and its university . . . . [T]o most people the name is all that is known of the man who first took up the reins of government in the newly created province of Alberta.[1]

Marzolf's thesis helped to dispel some of that obscurity, for it presented considerable biographical material about Dr. Rutherford and assessed his pioneer role in Alberta education. L. G. Thomas's analysis of Alberta's Liberal regime (1905–21), published in 1959, has also had time to reach a wider readership and present the role played by Rutherford in the early political life of the province, particularly his part in the climactic Alberta and Great Waterways debacle of 1910.[2]

Rutherford had not been completely neglected, however, for two events in the early 1950s brought him posthumous recognition and publicity. On 15 May 1951 a new library at the University of Alberta was formally opened and named the Rutherford Library in honour of the university's founder and long-time chancellor. In his address on that occasion, former university president R. C. Wallace (1928–1936) paid tribute to his friend and colleague:

I feel honoured in being asked to speak at the opening of this building. The occasion brings back to me memories that are very dear. The authorities of this University have decided to perpetuate the name of a former Chancellor, Dr. A. C. Rutherford, with whom I had the pleasure of being associated in a very intimate way during the years when he was Chancellor and I was President of this University. The University was very dear to Dr. Rutherford. The students were very dear to him. The tea in his hospitable home on the day before graduation to all the students who were to kneel before him on the following day was an event long to be remembered.

... He was a lover of books, and had acquired a library of Canadiana, which had few peers, among private collections. Not only had he the library, but he knew his books. Many students sought him to obtain assistance in some phase of Canadian studies. He could give the necessary references, and he could usually supply the necessary material out of his wealth of books and pamphlets and documents. So it is eminently fitting that the man who was the first Chancellor for many years of a University which he had much to do with the founding in his capacity as Premier, and as a great lover of books, should be associated for all time with this building, which so proudly carries his name. There is still a deeper reason why I feel happy in being present on this occasion. I had a great affection for Dr. Rutherford. His wisdom, his transparent sincerity, his kindliness and generous support won my heart. It is a special honour to pay this tribute to a man whose name will always live in the annals of this Province.[3]

Three years later the Geographic Board of Alberta named a 2,847-metre peak thirty-four kilometres northwest of Jasper, Mount Rutherford.[4] During Alberta's jubilee in 1955 radio and press coverage briefly identified the man after whom the mountain was named.[5]

On 29 May 1964, fifty-six years after her father had been so honoured by the same university, Mrs. Hazel McCuaig received the honorary degree of LL.D. from the University of Alberta. The citation referred to Dr. Rutherford's central role in the inauguration of the university, and paid tribute to Mrs. McCuaig's continuing devotion to the institution founded by her father:

Mrs. McCuaig was a student of arts in the early years and mother of children who have passed through the university. She inherited from her father an abiding affection for the University expressed through a continuing association with large numbers of undergraduates. For many years she has forwarded to some hundreds of women graduates an annual newsletter to keep them informed of their fellow students and of events at the University.

She has made available from time to time many interesting records and was responsible for donating to the University, her share of her father's valuable library of rare Canadiana.

She has been active in Church, social and charitable organizations in Edmonton, notably the Women's Canadian Club of which she is a Past President.

Mrs. McCuaig is being honoured today for her unwavering interest in the welfare of many hundreds of students who have gone forth from these halls to add lustre to their alma mater, for her loyalty and generosity to the University and for her exemplary public service.[6]

In 1967 the University of Alberta Rare Book Room published a catalogue of the Rutherford collection that included a biography of Rutherford. In 1973 the University Archives released a guide to the Rutherford Papers that also included a brief biography of the first premier.

Controversy, too, focussed public attention on Rutherford. From 1966 to 1970 the campaign to save Rutherford House introduced a new generation of Albertans to their first premier. The subsequent restoration of his home generated additional publicity, and the house itself has been a means of telling the Rutherford story to thousands of visitors since 1973.

On 27 September 1974 the new wing of Rutherford Library at the University of Alberta, designated Rutherford North, was officially opened by Mrs. Hazel McCuaig. The distinctive brick of Rutherford North had been specially designed by the Edmonton architectural firm of Minsos, Vaitkunas and Jamieson to conform in appearance with the original Rutherford Library. The new brick was named "Rutherford Autumn Leaf" and registered as such in the building industry.[7]

More recently, the government of Ontario, through the Ontario Heritage Foundation, recognized the achievements of one of its illustrious native sons. On 23 November 1985 a historical plaque was unveiled at the Osgoode Township Museum in Vernon, Ontario, near Rutherford's birthplace. The plaque text reads:

ALEXANDER CAMERON RUTHERFORD 1857–1941

The first premier of Alberta, Rutherford was born in Osgoode Township of Scottish parents and educated at McGill University. In 1895, after practising law in Ottawa and Kemptville, he moved to Strathcona, near Edmonton. Elected to the territorial assembly seven years later, Rutherford achieved prominence as deputy speaker of the legislature. When the province of Alberta was created in 1905, he became premier, provincial treasurer, and minister of education in the first government. Rutherford skillfully established the province's administrative, judicial, and educational framework, but prolonged debate regarding a controversial railway policy precipitated his resignation as premier in 1910. Although retired from politics after 1913, he retained an active interest in educational matters, serving as chancellor of the University of Alberta from 1927 until his death.[8]

Today, while Rutherford's contributions to Alberta are still not sufficiently appreciated, he clearly has an assured and prominent place in Alberta history. As a founding father of both a province and a university, his name will endure with them. But only an appreciation of his nearly half century of continuous public service at the local, territorial, and provincial levels can provide an adequate measure of his stature.

It was as a political figure that Rutherford made his most significant contributions to the province. During his eleven years in public office from 1902 to 1913, Rutherford displayed an amazing capacity for work and responsibility, tireless and serious dedication to the tasks he assumed, and intense loyalty to the province he helped to create. His central concern for public education was reflected in his government's generous financial support of the public school system, its education tax on land, and its establishment of the university and normal school, as well as in his attendance at the Imperial Education Conferences in London in 1907 and 1911. He took particular interest in providing public schools for new Canadians; supplying free, improved public school textbooks; establishing a system of public libraries, a provincial library, and archives; and building an adequate university library, to which he donated generously. These developments flowed from Rutherford's belief that education was the chief determining factor in character building, the basis of intelligent citizenship, and the foundation of all good government.[9] In 1929, when asked about the factors in his own success, Rutherford mentioned ambition, having a goal, and the will to work hard:

> Study is necessary all along the road; one must keep abreast of world thought and in pace with happenings in his own environment. There is little success in store for the laggard.[10]

Rutherford's political career exemplified his creed, not only in his eagerness to carry a heavy burden of responsibility, but in his government's legislation as well: the society it envisioned was not for laggards.

Descriptions of Premier Rutherford in 1907 and 1908 throw light on his personality and political style:

> In personal intercourse, the most striking characteristic of Mr. Rutherford is his simple straightforwardness. A big stalwart man, he moves quietly among his fellow townsmen with a friendly nod and a kind word for everybody. An honest, upright figure in politics, scarcely fifty years of age, he bids fair to enjoy a long lease of power.[11]

> Back of his cheery eyes and the almost benevolent lines of his face that expands readily to open-hearted laughter, there are lines of stubborn strength that have to be reckoned with by the man who would oppose him. Viking-like in his massive physique and straight-forward kindly manner, he is not a politician in the sense of a man of guile or tortuous intellect born to schemes for the advancement of self or party, but rather a man of action in the service of his country with a capacity for finding his task and setting to work on it with a directness of attack and simple earnestness before which obstacles cannot stand.

> His manner of democratic friendliness is a natural attribute of a man of this type. It is indeed no outcome of political training that the Premier of Alberta

is so approachable, so easily accessible to any citizen of his Province. When an interview has been given by him, the visitor invariably finds the Premier interested in his mission, and never too busy to hear it in detail.[12]

Politically, Rutherford was an individualist. He sought political office as an independent candidate in 1896, 1898, and 1902, and as an independent Liberal in 1913. In 1921 he campaigned for the Conservative party. Even as a leader of the Liberal party he twice appealed to the electorate more on the basis of principle and the welfare of the province than on the grounds of partisanship. When he opposed the Liberal government of Premier Sifton in the 1913 election, Rutherford did so as "a true Liberal," yet when he himself was opposed by Liberal followers in 1910, Rutherford felt betrayed. His approach to political issues was honest, sober, and cautious—too cautious for some of his ambitious, even reckless followers. His detractors found him staid, colourless, and uninspiring, unequipped for the cut and thrust of public debate; in a word, too gentlemanly. In him they found virtue, not charisma. Lacking guile himself, he could be hoodwinked, as he probably was by the promoters of the Alberta and Great Waterways Railway.

Rutherford was relatively inexperienced politically when the leadership of the Liberal party and, by virtue of that, the premiership as well were thrust upon him. During the next five years he revealed himself as the antithesis of a party "boss": he lacked toughness and cunning, cared little for partisan politics, and seemed almost surprised to be in the political arena at all. When the challenge to his leadership came in 1910, he appeared to have been taken completely unawares, suggesting that he was out of touch with his colleagues in the house. He took no decisive steps to protect his position but rather relied on a royal commission to find him innocent of any wrong-doing in the Alberta and Great Waterways agreement. But more than his propriety was in question; at issue was his fitness to lead the government, and, guilty or not, his challengers brought him down.

Monuments to his decisions during nearly five years of political power remain: the Alberta Government Telephone system; the location and even the style of the legislative building in Edmonton; the creation and location of the University of Alberta; and his second fine home, almost destroyed by the university he founded, but now an integral part of its landscape. Less tangible, but nonetheless significant, is the mass of founding legislation introduced by the Rutherford government from 1906 to 1910 that launched the new province on a stable course.

His concern for history, expressed in his own generously shared library and in his establishment of the university, the Historical Society of Alberta, and the public library system, made Rutherford more than anyone the founder of a historical tradition in Alberta. As Dr.L.G. Thomas noted recently in a tribute to Rutherford, he created a climate in which historical scholarship, both popular and academic, could be pursued.[13]

Though Rutherford's timing and siting of the university cost him heavily in legislative support, he himself always regarded the achievement as his finest. Men of lesser conviction might have been overwhelmed by the barrage of criticism that he resolutely endured. It was especially fitting that his final public act should have been to preside at convocation on 19 May 1941, just three weeks before his death. His fourteen years as chancellor of his beloved university was the fulfillment of thirty-five years of unwavering devotion to an ideal.

Individuality and idealism are suggested in Rutherford's early law practice as well. Unlike more ambitious colleagues, Rutherford encouraged prospective clients to settle disputes out of court; he took cases that others regarded as lost causes, and defended clients who could ill afford a lawyer's fee.

His long life was filled with a wide range of interests and activities. He collected and read one of the largest private libraries in Canada, especially in the fields of Canadian history and literature, and he generously opened his library to those who shared his interests. Rutherford was a devout Christian who devoted much of his energy and ability to the Baptist Church. It is significant that even during the hectic days when he was premier, he continued to serve as a deacon at the First Baptist Church in Strathcona. His willingness to serve in a multitude of community, fraternal, and special-interest organizations was characteristic of his entire adult life. This in itself represents a notable achievement. Rutherford enjoyed playing tennis until his later years, when he took up the less strenuous game of golf at the Mayfair Golf and Country Club. Only a week before his death, he played golf with his old friend the Hon. J. C. Bowen.[14] Fond of trees and plants, Rutherford spent many happy hours in his garden. Friendly and affable, he made his home a centre of social activity. Ironically, though he had a great many friends, Rutherford apparently had few intimates in his life.[15]

At the time of his death in June 1941, many prominent Albertans paid Rutherford tribute.[16] Premier Aberhart spoke of the idealism that characterized all of his undertakings; H. H. Parlee, chairman of the University of Alberta Board of Governors, referred to Rutherford as one of the builders of western Canada, whose nobility of character, honesty of purpose, genius, and vision made him one of Alberta's great pioneers. Edmonton's Mayor Fry said that Rutherford's attainments had formed a lasting chapter in the history of Alberta and western Canada. Rutherford's old colleague, Chief Justice Harvey,[17] concluded that

in his life both public and private he deserved and received the respect and esteem of all, and he has established a record that will always be a source of pride to the relatives and friends he has left behind.

At the funeral service for Dr. Rutherford, held at Strathcona Baptist Church on 13 June 1941, Donald E. Cameron, chief librarian at the University of Alberta, spoke of his friend with deep affection and insight:

There are many aspects of Dr. Rutherford's life of which one might fittingly speak now—of his life-long interest in Canadian literature and history; of his distinction as a collector; and of his unfailing courtesy and generosity to students who looked to him for sympathetic help in their studies. So too, of his character as a man many things might be said in which we should find ourselves in warm accord.

To know the man, something more than our daily contact with him is needed. Dr. Rutherford, be it remembered came of Highland Scottish ancestry.... The type to which he belonged is not too commonly found, nor is it too rare. It may be found in places high or low; high position does not corrupt its simplicity, nor does lowly place depress any element of its character. Some of its marks are steadfastness, unobtrusive conviction, tolerance, and great kindness. Behind the type as we discern it there lies often—usually, perhaps—a strong religious tradition, with varying degrees of a type of quietism that finds its peace remote from the controversies that sunder men.

The residual heritage from such a Scottish tradition can be just such a character as Dr. Rutherford manifested—its main mark, as it impressed itself on his fellowmen, being perhaps best described as a most gentle earnestness.[18]

Figure 72: Premier Rutherford, c. 1905 - 1910.
(Provincial Archives of Alberta, A.4396)

CHRONOLOGY

1857	February 2	A. C. Rutherford born at father's farm near Ormond, Canada West (Ontario).
1865	October 25	Mattie Birkett born at Ottawa.
1863-76		Attended school at Ormond, Metcalfe, and Woodstock.
1877		Taught school at Osgoode, Ontario.
1881		Graduated from McGill University (B.A., B.C.L.).
1881-85		Articled with Scott, McTavish & McCracken and O'Connor and Hogg, in Ottawa.
1885		Called to Ontario bar, began ten-year practice at Kemptville, Ontario, with Hodgins, Kidd and Rutherford.
1888	December 19	Married Mattie Birkett.
1890	October 4	Cecil Alexander Cameron Rutherford born.
1893	July 26	Hazel Elizabeth Rutherford born.
1894	August	Visited Edmonton and South Edmonton, N.W.T.
1895	June 10	Arrived at South Edmonton with his family.
1896	June	Appointed Secretary-Treasurer of South Edmonton School Board.
	August 4	Defeated in by-election for Edmonton seat in N.W.T. Legislative Assembly.
1897	February	Elected first worthy master of Acacia Lodge, A.F. & A. Masons.
1898	November 4	Defeated in general election for Edmonton seat in N.W.T. Legislative Assembly.

1899	June 27	Appointed first secretary-treasurer of Town of Strathcona (until 1906).
	July	Formed partnership with F. C. Jamieson.
1900	August	Elected president of the Strathcona Liberal Association.
1900	September - November	Supported Frank Oliver in federal general election campaign.
1902	May 21	Elected to N.W.T. Legislative Assembly for District of Strathcona.
1903	April	Elected deputy speaker by N.W.T. Legislative Assembly.
	September 4	Marjorie Cameron Rutherford born.
1905	January 21	Marjorie Cameron Rutherford died.
	August 2	Elected first president of the Alberta Liberal Association.
	August 23	Elected vice-president of the Provincial Lord's Day Alliance.
	August 29	Nominated Liberal candidate for the provincial riding of Strathcona.
	September 1	Alberta became a province.
	September 2	Sworn in as premier of Alberta.
	September 9	Gazetted as premier, minister of education, and provincial treasurer of Alberta.
	November 9	Led Liberals to twenty-three to two victory in first provincial election.
1906	March 15	First Legislature of Alberta opened at Thistle Rink, Edmonton.
	April 23	Introduced University Bill.
	September	A. T. Mode joined firm of Rutherford & Jamieson.
	October	Attended provincial premiers' conference at Ottawa.
1907	April 6	Announced that the university would be located at Strathcona.

	May - July	Attended Imperial Education Conference in London, visited Scotland, and toured Europe.
	September 26	Received honorary LL.D. degree from University of Toronto.
1907	October 13	Received honorary LL.D. degree from McMaster University.
	December	Elected vice-president of the Dominion Lord's Day Alliance.
1908	January 1	Dr. H. M. Tory began duties as president of University of Alberta.
	March	Dr. Rutherford and Dr. Tory attended first meeting of University of Alberta Senate as ex officio members.
	May - July	Cottage built at Banff for Dr. Rutherford.
	September 22	First classes at University of Alberta commenced, included Cecil Rutherford.
	October 13	Dr. Rutherford received honorary LL.D. from University of Alberta at first convocation.
	November	Elected president of Baptist Convention of Western Canada.
1909	February 24	Dr. Rutherford introduced railway guarantee bills in the Legislature.
	March 22	Led Liberals to thirty-seven to four victory in second provincial election.
	May	Bought half hectare lot adjoining University of Alberta site from L. Garneau.
	September 29	Turned the sod for the University of Alberta Arts Building.
	October 1	Assisted at the laying of the cornerstone for the Legislative Building.
	November 2	Excavation for new Rutherford House completed.
1910	February 10	J. R. Boyle gave notice in the Legislature of questions concerning the Alberta and Great Waterways Railway.

	February 14	Public Works Minister Cushing submitted his resignation.
	May	Foundation of Rutherford House poured.
	May 26	Premier Rutherford submitted his resignation.
1910	November	Charles H. Grant joined the firm of Rutherford and Jamieson. Dr. Rutherford opened an Edmonton office.
	November	Report of Royal Commission on the Alberta and Great Waterways Railway released for publication.
1911	January 30	Great Western Garment Co. incorporated, A.C. Rutherford vice-president.
	February	Rutherford family moved into their new house.
	March	Elected to the University of Alberta Senate. Appointed King's Counsel.
	April - June	Visited Britain and continental Europe, invited to attend coronation of King George V.
	July 13	Elected representative to the Baptist Union.
	August	Opposed Frank Oliver for the federal Liberal nomination in Edmonton.
1912	May 9	First Founder's Day Tea held at Rutherford House.
	July	Dr. Rutherford and Hazel visited Britain, attended a garden party at Windsor Castle.
1913	April 17	Defeated in the provincial election in South Edmonton.
1915		Elected president of the St. Andrew's Society (until 1918).
1916		Appointed director of the National Service Commission in Alberta (until 1918).
		Appointed honorary colonel of the 194th Battalion, Canadian Expeditionary Force.
	June 5	Cecil Rutherford married Helen Martin.
1919		Elected president of the Historical Society of Alberta (until 1941).

	April 5	Cecil Rutherford called to the Alberta bar.
	September 17	Hazel Rutherford married S. H. McCuaig in Rutherford House.
1920	September 30	Eric McCuaig born in Rutherford House.
1921	July	Dr. Rutherford campaigned for the Conservative party in the provincial election. United Farmers of Alberta defeated the Liberal government.
1922	February 22	Appointed president of the McGill Graduates' Society.
	September 22	Ruth McCuaig born.
1923		Law firm of Rutherford, Jamieson and Grant becomes Rutherford, Jamieson, Rutherford and McCuaig.
1924	August 25	Helen McCuaig born.
1926	April 6	Margaret Rutherford born.
	December 20	Harwood McCuaig born.
1927	May 20	Elected chancellor of the University of Alberta.
1931	May	Re-elected chancellor.
	October 14	Received honorary LL.D. degree from McGill University.
1935	May	Re-elected chancellor.
	May 6	Received the King's Jubilee Medal.
1937	May 12	Received the King's Coronation Medal.
1938		Suffered a stroke.
	December 19	Dr. and Mrs. Rutherford celebrated their golden wedding anniversary.
1939	May	Re-elected chancellor.
1940	September 13	Mattie Rutherford died in Rutherford House.
		Rutherford House sold to Delta Upsilon Fraternity.
1941	June 11	Dr. Rutherford died at the age of eighty-four.
1948	May 18	Eric McCuaig admitted to Alberta bar.

1951	May 15	Rutherford Memorial Library opened at University of Alberta.
1954	December 15	"Mount Rutherford" in Jasper National Park gazetted.
1957	October 22	Cecil Rutherford died.
1964	May 29	Hazel McCuaig received honorary LL.D. from University of Alberta.
1968	April	Delta Upsilon Fraternity sold Rutherford House to University of Alberta.
1969	May	Delta Upsilon Fraternity vacated Rutherford House.
1970	November	University of Alberta Board of Governors agreed to lease Rutherford House to provincial government.
1973	June 10	Restored Rutherford House opened to public.
1974	May 11	Rutherford House officially opened as historic house museum.
1974	September 27	New wing ("Rutherford North") of Rutherford Library officially opened by Mrs. Hazel McCuaig.
1979	June 28	Rutherford House designated a Provincial Historic Resource.
1983	May 21	Ruth Bate (nee McCuaig) died.
1984	February 25	Helen Rutherford (nee Martin) died.
1985	April	Friends of Rutherford House organized
1986	March 6	Stanley McCuaig died.
1988		Tea house opened in the den and sun porch.
		Delta Upsilon Visitors' Centre (boardroom and education area) completed in Rutherford House lower level.

APPENDIX A

Election Address by A. C. Rutherford, 1896[1]

Gentlemen: At the request of a large number of Electors, I have the honour to present myself as a candidate at the approaching bye-election for the representation of the Edmonton District in the Legislative Assembly of the North-West Territories.

The Edmonton District is one of the largest and most important in the Territories. It has heretofore been represented by able and representative men. I shall, if elected, endeavour to maintain the character of your past representation.

I desire to see the lands in the district cultivated and occupied. I desire the growth and prosperity of the district and the fullest development of its resources. An urgent request should be made to the Dominion Government for a more liberal appropriation for the purpose of opening communications to and through these lands by common roads. So long as the existing method of distributing the funds for the construction of roads and bridges prevails, I shall keep in view the welfare of the whole district, and see to the impartial distribution of the moneys placed at my disposal.

A liberal provision should be made for the maintenance of our schools, so that local taxation may bear as lightly as possible upon the people.

The procedure of our Courts and our Ordinances should be rendered as simple as possible, so as to avoid the danger of unnecessary litigation. The cost of legal proceedings has been reduced considerably within the past few years. A further reduction in this regard is necessary in connection with several matters.

The Legislature of the Territories has jurisdiction over many questions which affect the commercial interests, as well as the agricultural interests of the community. A revision of the Ordinances will be made in the year 1898. Should you select me as your representative, I shall be pleased to urge the adoption of any suggestions, from whatever source they may come, with a view to making our laws more perfect-- always keeping in view the welfare of the Territories in general, and the Edmonton District in particular.

It is impossible for me to make a personal canvas of the District, as the time before election day is short, but I will be pleased to have my friends exert themselves in my behalf. Should you favour me with your votes and influence, I shall do my utmost to merit your confidence. Your obedient servant, A. C. Rutherford.

1 Provincial Archives of Alberta, 75.518 (3).

APPENDIX B

Platform of the Alberta Liberal Convention, 1905[1]

Following is the platform adopted at the Provincial Liberal convention in Calgary on Thursday, August 3, 1905.

1   Resolved that this convention of the Liberals of the new Province of Alberta, having been called for the purpose of organizing a Provincial Liberal Association, and consisting of representatives from all parts of the Province, hereby expresses its adherence to those political principles which have ever characterized the Liberal or Reform party in Canada and elsewhere, and which consist in the conviction (1) that the intelligent opinion of the people is the true and just source of all political power; (2) that the administrators of public affairs should be under continued responsibility of the electorate; (3) that the true end of government is the promotion of the welfare of the masses of the people by the creation and preservation so far as it is possible by the action of the state, of equal opportunities in life for every individual, by the vigorous repression of all encroachments on the rights of the people on the part of monopolistic corporations, by amelioration of the conditions of life, and the redress of injustice, by a steady, orderly and progressive administration of affairs, and by watchful and continued attention to the wants of those new settlers whose courage, industry and thrift are creating the prosperity of the West.

2   Resolved that this convention adheres to the principle of Provincial rights, and is determined to maintain intact and unimpaired the full legislative and executive authority of the Province of Alberta under the constitution of Canada.

3   Resolved that this convention hereby declares its belief that the government of the new provinces should maintain an efficient system of common schools in order to meet the wants of the settler, and to extend to the children of all classes of the population an equal opportunity to obtain a good primary education, that this system should receive liberal financial assistance from the government revenues, and that all schools receiving such assistance and supported by taxation should be subject in every particular to the direct and continued supervision, regulation and control of the Provincial department of education.

1 Provincial Archives of Alberta, 69.199 (11).

4   Resolved that in all provincial legislation and administration the desirability of retaining or acquiring control of all provincial franchises should be kept steadily in view, and that while business enterprises should be recognized and promoted in every legitimate way, nevertheless no laws should be passed or acts done which would shackle the freedom of the people in respect thereto.

5   Resolved that inasmuch as the progress and prosperity of the Province will depend almost entirely upon the development of the agricultural and ranching industries, the provincial government should assist in every possible way and particularly by the establishment of a system of dairy instruction by encouraging cheese factories, creameries, forestry, and fruit growing, by assisting the farmers and farmers' associations to improve the breed of live stock of all kinds, by assisting agricultural fairs, by encouraging the full utilization of all farm products, and the preparation of such products for the market in the most condensed and remunerative form, by the collection and dissemination among the farmers and ranchers of the latest and fullest information as to the best available markets, and by extending to them every legitimate assistance in reaching those markets with the least possible loss of profit through excessive freight rates or the intervention of middlemen.

6   Resolved that this convention is in favour of a strong, economical and business administration of public affairs with prompt attention without unnecessary routine to the wants of the people in all parts of the Province.

7   Resolved that inasmuch as the true development of the Province and the prosperity of its citizens depends in very large measure upon the enjoyment of proper facilities in all parts of the country for easy access to markets, and inasmuch as the rapid influx of population and the establishment of new settlements render it impossible and also unwise that the new local improvement districts with their limited power of taxation should be called upon to provide such facilities without material assistance from provincial revenues, therefore this convention declares its belief that the Government should adopt without delay a vigorous and practical policy of bridging the more important streams and of maintaining a first-class system of main thoroughfares to all market towns, the cost of which should be largely met out of the public funds of the Province.

8   Resolved that inasmuch as the Provinces westward of the Great Lakes are peculiarly interested in the establishment of a new route to the seaboard alternative to that afforded by railways to the Atlantic coast, and inasmuch as the creation of two new Provinces out of the North-West Territories gives the first opportunity for co-operation with this end in view, therefore this convention is of the opinion that the earliest possible steps should be taken to secure joint action by the Governments of Manitoba, Saskatchewan, Alberta and British Columbia, in order to ascertain definitely and finally the feasibility of the Hudson's Bay route as an outlet for our commodities and to

decide upon the best method of constructing a railway by that route to tide-water, whereby the long land haul may be diminished by one half and the ocean voyage to European ports also materially decreased.

9   Resolved that this convention recognizes the great importance of the mining industry in the commercial life of this province and believes that the provincial government should foster and encourage this industry in every possible way.

10   Resolved that this convention regrets the necessity which existed for the introduction into the Alberta Act of a clause continuing the exemption of railway land from taxation; that this convention is in favour of the government urging upon the Federal authorities the advisability of removing the restrictions at as early a date as possible.

11   Resolved that this convention believes that the new Provincial Government should take the earliest possible steps to induce the Federal Government to set aside a sufficient part of the public domain as a permanent endowment for a Provincial University and an Agricultural College in connection therewith.

12   Resolved that inasmuch as the revenues provided for the province under the Alberta Act are sufficient to meet all the present requirements of the Province, and are subject to large increases from time to time in proportion to the growth of our population, this convention declares its belief that there should be no immediate necessity to incur any provincial public debt or to pledge, alienate or hypothecate the assets of the Province to meet any real public need.

13   Resolved that in all the municipal legislation of the new Province the Government should be careful to give full opportunity to municipalities to retain or acquire control of all public utilities whenever they desire to do so and to protect them in every possible way against the encroachments of private corporations.

14   Resolved that this convention hereby expresses its belief that in the establishment of all public institutions and the erection of all public buildings due attention should be paid to the requirements of all parts of the province and that in selecting locations for the same, the government should consider the public convenience and the quick dispatch of business.

15   Resolved that this convention believes in the vigorous administration of justice by a firm enforcement of the criminal law, and a simple and prompt method of protecting civil rights.

APPENDIX C

The Hon. A. C. Rutherford's Speech to the Address of His Honour the Lieutenant-Governor, 20 March 1906[1]

Mr. Speaker, I wish to offer a few observations on the motion now before the House re the Address of His Honour the Lieutenant-Governor of the Province. In the first place let me congratulate the mover [Charles A. Stuart] of the address upon his very able effort. He delivered an address which is indeed a gem, and an address that would be well received, and would be fitting to deliver in any of the Houses of Parliament within the British realm. The Hon. Member for Gleichen no doubt will make his mark in this House and in the Province. Allow me also to congratulate the Hon. Member for Lacombe [W. F. Puffer] for his very practical address, and I have no doubt but what his advice will be very valuable to the members of this House. I feel also like congratulating the Honourable Leader of the Opposition, the Member for High River, [Albert J. Robertson] upon his address, and upon his elevation to the leadership of his Majesty's Loyal Opposition in this House, and hope he may long hold that honour. His address was well delivered, and with the tone of his address I have very little fault to find. Of course I took exception to some of his deductions and observations, and I shall take occasion to treat with some of the observations made. The Hon. Leader of the Opposition found some fault with the address of His Honour the Lieutenant-Governor, and took some exception to what he called omissions in the address. As you will see Mr. Speaker, from the address of His Honour, we have quite a bill of fare to present to this House, and this is the first session of the first legislature of the Province of Alberta, and the Government felt it was their duty to lay the foundations in this new Province with every care and wisdom, and you will find that the Government measures are prepared with a wise end in view. Of course we cannot mention all that we have done and propose to do within the brief limits of an address at the opening of a legislature, but Mr. Speaker, the Hon. Member for High River mentioned as omissions in the address the matter of the Hudson Bay Railway and of the C.P.R. exemptions. With regard to the Hudson Bay Railway I fully agree, and I am pleased that the Leader of the Opposition agrees with the Government that it will be to the great advantage of the people of this western Province to have a railway constructed to Hudson Bay so as to give an outlet for this western Province to the European markets, with much less cost than to go by way of Montreal. I might inform you, Mr. Speaker, that we are gathering all the information we can to determine the

1 Provincial Archives of Alberta, 75.518 (6).

feasibility of the Hudson Bay route, with a view to obtaining all the information we can as to the navigability of the Hudson Bay route, and from the information gathered I believe the Hudson Bay is navigable for at least four or five months in the year. As soon as we have all the necessary information we will take up the matter with our sister Province Saskatchewan with a view to pushing the matter of the Hudson Bay Railway as soon as possible. I might mention that the Canadian Northern Railway Company have surveyors in the field now, with a view to constructing a line to Hudson Bay. We hope the Dominion Government will also give some encouragement to the construction of this line of railway, and I believe they will (applause). The Government of our sister Province of Saskatchewan takes the stand I believe that the Dominion Government should give every encouragement for the construction of the Hudson Bay Railway. I feel the importance of this matter, and Mr. Speaker, the House may rest assured that the Government of this Province will do everything in their power with a view to promoting same.

The Hon. Member for High River, Mr. Speaker, also took exception that His Honour in the address from the throne did not mention anything in regard to the C.P.R. exemptions. My view of the treatment of this matter is that this House should pass an address calling upon the Dominion Government to endeavour to negotiate with the C.P.R. Co. with a view to the doing away of these exemptions. It is a hardship upon the settlers of this country that there is so much property belonging to the C.P.R. and other railway corporations exempt from taxation, and these exemptions should be removed at as early a date as possible. Further, Mr. Speaker, the Government is also considering the matter of the taxation of the C.P.R. and also all other railway companies. If we are not in a position to place legislation before you at this session, I think it will be our duty to place legislation before this House at the second session with a view to having railway companies taxed; with a view also to taxing all other corporations, such as banks and insurance companies, and we might also very well consider the matter of the taxation of the output of coal. But Mr. Speaker, I think this question of taxation should be considered very carefully and we should give this matter due consideration so as not to set back the prosperity of this country. Matters should be carefully considered. The older Provinces of Canada place a tax upon a few corporations, and I think it is up to us to consider the matter of following along the same lines.

The Hon. Leader of the Opposition dealt with the result of the recent elections in this Province, which occurred on the 9th November last. I might state that the result of that election could not prove otherwise but a source of deep gratification to me, and a source of gratification to the Government, but at the same time I took exception to the remarks of the Hon. Leader of the Opposition as to the causes of our victory of the 9th November (applause). Our victory was indeed a sweetened one, because we have not only a majority in the House, but a large majority amounting to 6000 of the popular vote (loud applause).

The Hon. Leader of the Opposition, Mr. Speaker, cited several causes for the lack of success of the opposition; one was that the Dominion Government interfered in the elections with their officials. I found in the campaign that the two Conservative members of the House of Commons for Alberta took an active part in those elections, but do not know when those two members took that stand why the two Liberal members of the House of Commons should not have been active for us (applause). I did not find in the constituency that I have the honour to represent that the Dominion Government officials were active in my behalf. I do not know that they required to be active, but I found on the other hand that some of the old territorial government officials, that might be classed as our own officials, were active agents in opposition to myself and other government candidates (applause).

The Hon. Leader of the Opposition cited as one of the causes for the defeat of the Conservative party in this Province, the matter of misrepresentation upon the part of Liberal candidates, and on the part of Liberals especially in connection with our school system. My experience was that the misrepresentation and exaggeration was all on the other side (applause). On my own part I largely took the school law as it is, and almost entirely devoted my attention to the reading of the various clauses of the school ordinance, such as we have in the Province to-day, so that in following that course, so that in following that course [sic], no charge could be made against us of misrepresentation in connection with the school ordinance. To my mind, Mr. Speaker, to-day we have the best school ordinance that exists in any of the Provinces of this Dominion of Canada (hear, hear and applause). Our school law has worked out well, and it is working out well in our Province of Alberta to-day, and I have failed to hear any of our opponents cite in any respect wherein our school law could be amended.

The Hon. Leader of the Opposition cited also as one of the causes for defeat the matter of the expenditure of public moneys in the various constituencies under the direction of Liberal candidates, or rather the promise of big expenditures in the various constituencies. I do not think, Mr. Speaker, when we came into power that the big wheels of Government should stand still. I found, right on the commencement, school districts had to be formed, and found also that there was occasion for improvement of roads and construction of bridges, and occasion found to carry on the work of all the departments of the Government as it had been begun that season by the old territorial administration, and did not feel that it was intended that everything should stand still, as we were a business government, and would have been recreant to the great trust reposed upon us as a business administration if we had failed to see that all necessary works that had been commenced earlier in the season were not completed in a proper manner and in good time.

With regard to the location of the capitol, I beg leave to offer a few remarks. These remarks are occasioned by the remarks of the Hon. Leader of the Opposition yesterday, and I might say that during the election campaign I said very little in regard to the location of the capitol, and I would like to point out, Mr. Speaker, that the present policy of the Leader of the Opposition is out of harmony with the policy of the opposition enunciated in convention assembled at Red Deer. At the convention one of the planks adopted in their platform was that the location of the capitol should be left to the members of this House. I might add, Mr. Speaker, that previous to that convention I stated that my own feelings in the matter were that the location of the capitol should be left to the members, who would compose the first legislature of this Province, and an opportunity will be given some time this session for any of the members, who wish to do so, to advocate the claims of any place which they may see fit should be the capitol of this fair Province. The opportunity will be given to the members to discuss this matter and vote as they wish on the question.

I do not propose on this occasion to explain the various government measures foreshadowed in the speech from the throne. These measures will come up and be discussed in detail during the progress of the session after the bills are printed, and have received second reading. It is expected of us that we shall lay, as before stated, a good foundation in this Province of Alberta. We have a great Province, one of the grandest Provinces in this fair Dominion of Canada. It is large in area, and it contains many valuable minerals and very fertile soil. No doubt millions of people will make this their home. Thousands of people are coming to our land from every clime, and it will be our duty to attend to the wants of those people so far as it may be in our power. It will be our duty to see that schools are established in the various new districts. It will be our duty to consider the question of good roads and the construction of bridges so that an opportunity will be given the settlers to reach market towns. After all, the best immigration agent that we can have is the settler, and we should consider having good schools, roads and bridges, and it will be at least part of our duty in administering to the wants of the people who may come to our Province, in order to have a contented and happy people within our domain. The class of immigration coming to this country is indeed satisfactory, and many in good circumstances. The early settlers, the pioneers of this Province, came here with very little; they came largely to improve their circumstances, and mostly every new settler comes with that end in view, and it is a source of gratification that the early settlers are doing well. The foreign immigrants are doing well, and obtaining excellent results, and it is a source of gratification that they are desirous of having schools formed in their midst.

I am sure, Mr. Speaker, it will be a source of pleasure to members of the House that we will have a visit from Prince Arthur of Connaught during the session. It will be the duty of this House to present an address and entertain him in some way. This visit will be at a most opportune time, and will strengthen indeed, if it requires any strengthening, the bands of unity of this Canada of ours and the motherland.

The speech from the throne refers to the encouragement which we are giving, and propose to give to the agricultural interests of the Province. We find that quite a number of butter factories existed in the Province, and it was expected that the Government should take over these factories. We have done so, not on our own motion altogether. We found that the farmers were desirous that the Provincial Government should operate them, and we propose to carry on operations so long as it is in the best interests of the Province that we should do so, and I do not think that the Province will be out anything, if at all, very little in connection with same. I understand Mr. Speaker there are quite a number of demands for establishment of new factories in the Province, and it will be our duty to meet the demands made upon us in this respect.

I had occasion to visit southern Alberta a few months ago, and I can say the southern country was a revelation to me. I found there that during the past season they had magnificent fields of grain in that country. It was a source of gratification and a source of pleasure to me to see the great advancement made in southern Alberta. Reference was made yesterday to what we might expect from the northern part of the Province. I hope and fully believe that there is a great future for northern Alberta. We know pretty well all what we can expect from this central part of the Province. It is much better known than other portions of this Province. I have stated that we propose encouragement to the agricultural interests of the Province to as great [an] extent that we possibly can. The attention of the Government was drawn a very short time ago to the advisability of encouraging the growing of beets for the manufacture of sugar. We find that the factories situated in Raymond are working under peculiar conditions, and it might perhaps be desirable that we should give them some encouragement by way of bonus, but I do not think the Government will deal with the matter of bonusing, as it should have careful consideration as the farmers who grow the beets must be recognized and the money not all given to the factories. This matter will be brought to the attention of the Department of Agriculture, and the Government will be pleased to receive suggestions in this matter. It is a comparatively new industry and it ought to be a growing industry in this Province.

We have appointed comparatively large committees for this House. We expect to receive suggestions through these committees. They were not appointed to do nothing, and we expect them to be active, and they will from time to time report to this House what should be done to the advantage of the Province. Right here let me state that the Government measures are pretty well ready for this session. We introduced yesterday five bills and to-day nine, and a number more will be introduced in the course of a few days. I understand there will be a large number of private bills for introduction during the course of the session, and I must impress upon the members the desirability of having them ready for presentation to the House at the earliest possible date. If the Government is to do their part in having business ready for the House, we hope the members will have their bills ready so we may have employment during the session from the beginning. We are all busy men, and while we should have our legislation as perfect as possible to give it every consideration, yet it is necessary that we should be a working body, and have the business transacted in a business way (applause). We have, as I stated, a grand Province, one of the grandest in this Dominion. We have an excellent subsidy given us for the carrying on of our duties in this Province, by the Dominion Government. I believe we will have sufficient revenues to carry on the business of the country for many years without being under the necessity of borrowing money. I do not say we are getting too great a subsidy from the Dominion Government. We can very well spend all the revenues we receive (hear, hear and applause).

Now, Mr. Speaker, I have touched upon a few of the matters mentioned in the speech of His Honour the Lieutenant-Governor, and I shall have occasion to speak at greater length some other time during the session. In this first session probably a little advice might not be taken amiss, and I would be pleased to see every member take a deep interest in the session. Very nearly all of us will be making their maiden addresses this session, and I hope each member will endeavour to do his part to make a success of his duties in the Legislative Halls of this great Province of Alberta.

APPENDIX D

Statutes of the Province of Alberta, 1906–1910[1]

A. *Passed in the First Session of the First Legislative Assembly, 1906*

Chap.

* * 1. An Act for granting to His Majesty certain sums of money required for defraying certain expenses of Civil Government from the First day of September, 1905, to the Thirty-first day of December, 1905, and for other purposes

* * 2. An Act for granting to His Majesty certain sums of money for the Civil Service for the Financial Year ending the Thirty-first day of December, 1906, and for a portion of 1907, and for other purposes relating thereto

* * 3. An Act respecting the Statutes

* * 4. An Act respecting the Public Service

* * 5. An Act respecting the Treasury Department and the Auditing of the Public Accounts

* 6. An Act respecting the Department of the Attorney General

* 7. An Act respecting the Deparment of the Provincial Secretary

* 8. An Act respecting the Department of Agriculture

* * 9. An Act respecting Public Printing

* 10. An Act respecting Public Works

* 11. An Act to amend Chapter 24 of the Ordinances of the North-West Territories 1903 (Second Session), intituled "An Ordinance respecting Local Improvement Districts"

* 12. An Act to amend Chapter 25 of the Ordinances of the North-West Territories, 1901, intituled "An Ordinance respecting Villages"

* 13. An Act respecting Police Magistrates and Justices of the Peace

* 14. An Act respecting Commissioners to Administer Oaths

---

1 Alberta, *Statutes of the Province of Alberta* (Edmonton, Government Printer), 1906–1910. Acts introduced by Premier Rutherford are designated by asterisks (*).

*15. An Act respecting Coroners

16. An Act respecting Notaries Public

*17. An Act respecting Sheriffs and Deputy Sheriffs

18. An Act respecting Clerks and Deputy Clerks

19. An Act respecting the Transfer and Descent of Land

20. An Act respecting Suits against the Crown by Petition of Right

21. An Act for the benefit of Mechanics and Labourers

22. An Act respecting the Dental Association of Alberta

23. An Act respecting Steam Boilers

24. An Act respecting Real Property in the Province of Alberta

*25. An Act to make regulations with respect to Coal Mines

26. An Act to regulate the speed and operation of Motor Vehicles on highways

27. An Act to prevent Frauds and Perjuries in relation to sales of Real Property

28. An Act respecting the Medical Profession

29. An Act to amend Chapter 29 of the Ordinances of the North-West Territories 1903 (Second Session), intituled "An Ordinance for the Protection of Game."

*30. An Act to supplement the revenues of the Crown in the Province of Alberta

31. An Act empowering Municipalities to establish and operate Telephone systems

32. An Act to amend Chapter 22 of the Ordinances of the North-West Territories 1900, intituled "An Ordinance respecting Brands"

33. An Act to amend Chapter 87 of the Consolidated Ordinances of the North-West Territories 1898, intituled "An Ordinance for the prevention of Prairie and Forest Fires"

34. An Act to amend Chapter 80 of The Consolidated Ordinances of the North-West Territories 1898, intituled "An Ordinance respecting Estray Animals"

35. An Act to Incorporate The Edmonton and Athabasca Development Company

36. An Act to amend Chapter 43 of the Ordinances of the North-West Territories 1900, intituled "The Edmonton Public Hospital"

*37. An Act respecting the encouragement of the Sugar Beet industry

38. An Act to amend Chapter 2 of The Consolidated Ordinances of the North-West Territories 1898, intituled "An Ordinance respecting the Legislative Assembly of the Territories"

39. An Act to amend Chapter 42 of the Ordinances of the North-West Territories 1901, intituled "An Ordinance to Incorporate the Town of Red Deer"

40. An Act to amend Chapter 4 of the Ordinances of the North-West Territories 1902, intituled "An Ordinance respecting Public Health"

41. An Act to incorporate the City of Wetaskiwin

*42. An Act to establish and incorporate a University for the Province of Alberta

43. An Act to incorporate the Alberta Association of Architects

*44. An Act to incorporate the St. Andrew's Society of Edmonton

*45. An Act to amend the Strathcona Radial Tramway Ordinance 1904

*46. An Act to incorporate The Strathcona Club of the Town of Strathcona

47. An Act to repeal Ordinance No. 28 of the Ordinances of the North-West Territories 1904, intituled "An Ordinance to Incorporate The English Club"

48. An Act to incorporate The Alberta Oil, Coal and Wheat Railway Company

49. An Act to incorporate The Kootenay, Alberta and Athabasca Railway Company

50. An Act to incorporate The Vermilion and Cold Lake Railway Company

51. An Act to incorporate The Edmonton and Athabasca Railway Company

52. An Act to incorporate The Alberta Southern Railway Company

53. An Act to incorporate The Alberta North-Western Railway Company

54. An Act to incorporate The Western Oil and Coal Consolidated

55. An Act to amend the Ordinances relating to the City of Calgary and to confirm certain by-laws of the said City and to Consolidate the Floating Debt

56. An Act respecting certain kinds of contemplated municipal public works for the Town of Macleod

57. An Act respecting Veterinary Surgeons

58. An Act to incorporate The Alberta Pacific Elevator Company (Limited)

59. An Act respecting The Alberta Canadian Insurance Company

60. An Act respecting The Wawanesa Mutual Insurance Company

61. An Act to incorporate the High River Club

62. An Act to amend Chapter 39 of the Ordinances of the North-West Territories 1903 (Second Session), intituled "An Ordinance to incorporate the Western Canada College"

63. An Act to incorporate the City of Medicine Hat

*64. An Act to incorporate the City of Lethbridge

65. An Act respecting the Occidental Fire Insurance Company

66. An Act intituled "An Act to incorporate The South Alberta Club"

67. An Act to incorporate The Red Deer Club

68. An Act to incorporate The Pincher Creek Club

69. An Act to confirm a certain by-law of the Town of St. Albert

70. An Act to amend Chapter 89 of The Consolidated Ordinances of the North-West Territories 1898, intituled "An Ordinance respecting the sale of Intoxicating Liquors and the issue of Licenses therefor"

71. An Act to amend Chapter 35 of the Ordinances of the North-West Territories 1904, intituled "An Ordinance to Incorporate the Investors' Guarantee Corporation of Canada"

72. An Act to amend Ordinance No. 43 of the North-West Territories 1901, intituled "An Ordinance to Incorporate the Town of Cardston"

73. An Act to incorporate The Empire Club

74. An Act to incorporate The Edelweiss Club

75. An Act for the relief of Daniel W. Henderson and Lloyd Austin

76. An Act to amend the Edmonton Charter

B. *Passed in the Second Session of the First Legislative Assembly, 1907*

Chap.

* 1. An Act for granting to His Majesty certain sums of money for the Civil Service for the Financial year ending the Thirty-first day of December, 1907, and for a portion of 1908

2. An Act respecting Controverted Elections

3. An Act respecting the Supreme Court

4. An Act respecting the District Courts

5. An Act to amend the Statute Law

* 6. An Act respecting Assignments and Preferences by Insolvent Persons

7. An Act respecting Insane Persons

8. An Act to further amend Chapter 89 of The Consolidated Ordinances of The North-West Territories 1898, intituled "An Ordinance respecting the Sale of Intoxicating Liquors and the issue of Licenses therefor"

10. An Act respecting Villages

11. An Act respecting Local Improvements

12. An Act respecting Public Health

13. An Act respecting the Registration of Births, Marriages and Deaths

14. An Act for the Protection of Game

15. An Act respecting Noxious Weeds

16. An Act respecting the Manufacture of Butter and Cheese

*17. An Act to Provide for the Establishment of Public Libraries

*18. An Act respecting the Taxation of Land for Educational Purposes

*19. An Act respecting the Taxation of Corporations and Others

20. An Act respecting the Legal Profession in Alberta and to establish the Law Society in the Province of Alberta

21. An Act respecting King's Counsel and Precedence at the Bar

22. An Act to amend Chapter 38 of The Consolidated Ordinances of the North-West Territories 1898, intituled "An Ordinance respecting the Holding of Lands in Trust for Religious Societies and Congregations"

23. An Act to incorporate the Historical Society of Alberta

24. An Act to amend Chapter 50 of the Statutes of 1906, intituled "An Act to incorporate the Vermilion and Cold Lake Railway Company"

25. An Act respecting the Diamond Railway Company, Limited

26. An Act to incorporate the Calgary and Knee Hill Railway Company

27. An Act to incorporate the Knee Hill Railway Company

28. An Act to incorporate the Crow's Nest and Prairie Electric Railway Company

29. An Act to incorporate the Red Deer Railway and Power Company

30. An Act to incorporate the Lethbridge Radial Tramway Company

*31. An Act to amend the Strathcona Radial Tramway Ordinance 1904

32. An Act to amend Ordinance No. 33 of 1893 and other Legislation respecting the City of Calgary

33. An Act to validate and confirm certain By-laws of the City of Calgary

*34. An Act to incorporate the City of Strathcona

35. An Act to further amend the Edmonton Charter

36. An Act to confirm certain By-laws of the City of Edmonton and a certain Agreement entered into between the Grand Trunk Pacific Railway Company and the City of Edmonton

37. An Act to amend Ordinance No. 43 of the Ordinances of the North-West Territories 1901, intituled "An Ordinance to incorporate the Town of Cardston"

38. An Act to amend Ordinance No. 29 of the Ordinances of the North-West Territories 1892, intituled "An Ordinance to incorporate the Town of Macleod", and to amend the Macleod Municipal Public Works Act

39. An Act to confirm a certain By-law of the Town of Fort Saskatchewan and a certain agreement between the said town and one Ormond Higman

40. An Act respecting the Young Men's Christian Association of Edmonton

41. An Act to incorporate the Elks' Club of Calgary

42. An Act to incorporate the Elks' Club of Edmonton

43. An Act to incorporate the Grand Lodge of Alberta of the Independent Order of Odd Fellows

44. An Act to incorporate the Life Underwriters' Association of Alberta

45. An Act to incorporate the Calgary Fire Insurance Company

46. An Act to amend Chapter 30 of the Ordinances of the North-West Territories 1904, intituled "An Ordinance to incorporate the Sisters of Mercy of the North-West Territories"

47. An Act to incorporate the Lacombe General Hospital of Lacombe

48. An Act to amend Ordinance No. 27 of the Ordinances of the North-West Territories 1889, No. 4 of 1891 and No. 31 of 1895, intituled "The Medicine Hat General Hospital Ordinance"

49. An Act respecting the Methodist Church

C. *Passed in the Third Session of the First Legislative Assembly, 1908*

Chap.

* 1. An Act for Granting to His Majesty certain sums of money for the Civil Service for the Financial Year ending the Thirty-first day of December, 1908, and for a portion of 1909

* 2. An Act respecting Inquiries concerning Public Matters

* 3. An Act respecting the Remission of certain Penalties

4. An Act respecting Constables

5. An Act respecting Partnerships

6. An Act respecting The Imperial Debtors' Act, 1869

7. An Act respecting the Enforcement of Judges' Orders in Matters not in Court

* 8. An Act to provide for the Garnishment of the Salaries of Civil Servants

9. An Act to expedite the decision of Constitutional and other Legal Questions

*10. An Act respecting Security to be given by Public Officers

11. An Act respecting the Alberta Industrial School for Boys

12. An Act with respect to Compensation to Workmen for Injuries suffered in the course of their Employment

*13. An Act to grant certain powers to the Minister of Education

14. An Act respecting Government Telephone and Telegraph Systems

15. An Act respecting Gaols and Prisons

*16. An Act respecting Mechanics' and Literary Institutes

17. An Act to amend the Coal Mines Act for the purpose of Limiting Hours of Work Below Ground

18. An Act respecting Drainage

19. An Act respecting Poisons

20. An Act to amend The Statute Law

21. An Act respecting Seed Grain

22. An Act to Incorporate the Grand Lodge of Alberta, Ancient, Free and Accepted Masons

23. An Act to amend the Lethbridge Charter

24. An Act to Incorporate the Harmonie Club

25. An Act to Incorporate the Calgary Young Men's Christian Association

26. An Act relating to the Town of Magrath

27. An Act to confirm By-law No. 34 of the Town of Raymond and to legalize a certain Agreement between the Town of Raymond and the Knight Sugar Company, Limited

28. An Act to Incorporate the Bow River Collieries Railway Company

29. An Act to amend Chapter 53 of the Statutes of 1906 of the Province of Alberta, being An Act to Incorporate the Alberta North-Western Railway Company

30. An Act to amend Chapter 39 of the Statutes of Alberta, 1906, -- An Act respecting the Town of Red Deer, amending Chapter 42 of the Ordinances of the North-West Territories 1901

31. An Act to Incorporate the Camrose Canadian Club

32. An Act to amend the Edmonton Charter

33. An Act respecting the Edmonton Radial Tramway

34. An Act to validate and confirm certain By-laws of the City of Edmonton

35. An Act to provide a system of Taxation for the Town of Daysland

36. An Act to amend Ordinances and Statutes respecting the City of Calgary

37. An Act for the relief of Western Canada College

38. An Act to Incorporate the Scandinavian Hospital in Wetaskiwin

39. An Act to Incorporate the Carbon Hill Railway Company

*40. An Act to amend the Strathcona Charter

41. An Act to authorize Robert Woods to practise Medicine

42. An Act to validate and confirm certain By-laws of the City of Wetaskiwin

43. An Act to authorize and empower the Village of Frank to construct an electric and power plant and to borrow the sum of Ten Thousand dollars for such purpose

D. *Passed in the Fourth Session of the First Legislative Assembly, 1909*

Chap.

* 1. An Act for Granting to His Majesty certain sums of Money for the Civil Service for the financial year ending the Thirty-first day of December, 1909

2. An Act respecting the Legislative Assembly of Alberta

3. An Act respecting Elections of Members of the Legislative Assembly

4. An Act to amend the Statute Law (Part I)

* 5. An Act to further amend the Statute Law (Part II)

6. An Act respecting Arbitration

7. An Act respecting Constables

8. An Act respecting the Liability of Municipal and other Public Corporations upon Debentures sold at a discount

9. An Act respecting Appeals from Assessments in Cities and Towns

*10. An Act respecting Official Auditors

11. An Act respecting Sheriffs and Deputy Sheriffs

12. An Act for the protection of Neglected and Dependent Children

13. An Act for the Payment of Wolf Bounty

*14. An Act to Authorize the Guarantee of Certain Securities of the Canadian Northern Railway Company

*15. An Act to Authorize the Guarantee of Certain Securities of the Grand Trunk Pacific Branch Lines Company

*16. An Act to provide for an Issue of Guaranteed Securities of the Alberta and Great Waterways Railway Company

17. An Act to amend the Lethbridge Charter

18. An Act to Validate and Confirm By-law Number 38 of the Town of Camrose

19. An Act to amend An Act to incorporate the Calgary Fire Insurance Company, being Chapter 45 of the year 1907

20. An Act to Incorporate The Alpine Club of Canada

*21. An Act to amend the Strathcona Charter

22. An Act respecting the Galt Hospital

23. An Act to Incorporate the Merchants Fire Insurance Company

24. An Act respecting Vermilion Centre School District to Legalize Assessments and Rates

25. An Act to amend Ordinances and Statutes respecting the City of Calgary, and to Validate and Confirm Certain By-laws of the said City

26. An Act to Incorporate The Cardston Club

27. An Act to Incorporate The Fairview Cemetery Company

28. An Act to further amend the Edmonton Charter, the various Acts amending the same, and the Edmonton Radial Tramway Act

29. An Act respecting the Town of Lacombe

30. An Act to Relieve Ner. D. Steele from Certain Legal Doubts as to his standing as a Physician and Surgeon

31. An Act to Incorporate The Sisters of Charity of The Providence General Hospital

32. An Act to Incorporate Les Filles de la Providence

33. An Act to Incorporate Les Filles de Jesus

*34. An Act to amend Chapter 32, 1895, of the Ordinances of the North-West Territories

35. An Act to Incorporate Les Reverends Pères de Sainte Marie de Tinchebray

36. An Act to amend An Act to incorporate the City of Wetaskiwin and to Validate, Confirm and amend By-law Number 103 of the said City

37. An Act to Incorporate The Royal Collieries Railway Company

38. An Act to Incorporate The Pincher Creek and Southern Railway Company

39. An Act to amend Chapter 29 of the Statutes of Alberta, 7 Edward VII, incorporating The Red Deer Railway Company

40. An Act to Incorporate The Southern Alberta Railway Company

41. An Act respecting The Calgary and Knee Hill Railway Company

42. An Act to Incorporate The Strathcona Central Railway Company

43. An Act to amend Chapter 54 of the Statutes of 1906 of the Province of Alberta, being An Act to incorporate the Western Oil and Coal Consolidated

44. An Act to Incorporate The Kootenay and Alberta Railway Company

45. An Act to Incorporate The Alberta Midland Railway Company

*46. An Act to Incorporate The Alberta and Great Waterways Railway Company

47. An Act to further amend Chapter 53 of the Statutes of 1906, Alberta, being An Act to incorporate the Alberta North Western Railway Company, as amended by Chapter 29 of the Statutes of 1908

48. An Act to Incorporate Lacombe and Blindman Valley Electric Railway Company

49. An Act to Incorporate The Lacombe, Bullocksville and Alix Electric Railway Company

50. An Act to empower McGillivray Creek Coal and Coke Company, Limited, to Construct a Tramway

51. An Act to amend Chapter 48 of the Statutes of 1906 of the Province of Alberta, being An Act to incorporate the Alberta Oil, Coal and Wheat Railway Company

E. *Passed in the First Session of the Second Legislative Assembly, 1910*

Chap.

* 1. An Act for Granting to His Majesty certain sums of Money for the five months ending the Thirty-first day of May, 1910

2. An Act respecting Land Surveyors

3. An Act to validate and confirm certain by-laws of the City of Calgary

* 4. An Act to validate and confirm certain by-laws of the City of Strathcona

5. An Act to confirm certain by-laws of the City of Edmonton and a certain agreement entered into between the Canadian Pacific Railway Company, the Calgary and Edmonton Railway Company and the City of Edmonton

6. An Act to validate and confirm certain by-laws of the Town of Cardston

7. An Act to ratify certain money by-laws of the City of Lethbridge and to amend its Charter

8. An Act to validate and confirm by-laws numbers fifty and sixty-one of the Town of Camrose

9. An Act to empower the Town of Claresholm to increase its borrowing powers

10. An Act to grant additional powers to the Town of Raymond for the purpose of acquiring or constructing public utilities

11. An Act to extend the borrowing powers of the Town of High River

12. An Act to grant additional powers to the Town of Taber for the purpose of acquiring or installing certain public utilities and to increase its borrowing power

13. An Act to incorporate the High River General Hospital of High River

14. An Act to amend Chapter 41 of the Statutes of Alberta of 1907, intituled "An Act to incorporate the Elks' Club of Calgary"

15. An Act respecting the Salvation Army

16. An Act respecting the Great West Permanent Loan Company

17. An Act respecting the Diamond Coal Company, Limited

18. An Act to incorporate the Alberta and Saskatchewan Central Railway Lines

19. An Act to incorporate the Lacombe and Brazeau Railway Company

20. An Act to amend the Act of incorporation of the Carbon Hill Railway Company, and for other purposes

21. An Act to amend Chapter 28 of the Statutes of Alberta, 1908

NOTES

Chapter I – Include inclusive text page numbers

1. The four children were Grace, fifteen; Peter, thirteen; Donald (called Daniel), eleven; James, seven. Another daughter was born in 1861 and named Jessie in memory of a previous daughter who had died in Scotland. A. D. Marzolf, "Alexander Cameron Rutherford and his Influence on Alberta's Educational Program" (M.Ed. thesis, University of Alberta, 1961), 5.

2. Ibid. Strict Protestant doctrine, individualism, and congregational autonomy characterized both churches.

3. Rutherford Papers, University of Alberta Archives (hereafter cited as U.A.A.), biographical note.

4. Marzolf, 6.

5. *Edmonton Journal*, 14 May 1929.

6. The firm was later called Kidd, Rutherford and Blanchet. Rutherford Papers, U.A.A.

7. Marzolf, 7.

8. Personal communication, Mrs. Hazel McCuaig.

9. Mrs. Hazel McCuaig believes that her mother's formal Christian name was Martha. Mrs. Helen Rutherford, on the other hand, believed that "Mattie" was the diminutive of Mathilda.

10. Cecil Rutherford's birthdate is often given as 4 October 1891, but the date recorded by Mrs. Rutherford in her Bible and on Cecil's passport and grave marker is 1890.

11. Marzolf and others mention the late 1880s as the time of Rutherford's visit in the West. Mrs. Hazel McCuaig believes that her father did go west, as far as British Columbia, in connection with a case at this earlier date. It was Rutherford's visit in 1894, however, that enabled him to establish so swiftly in South Edmonton the following year.

12. Marzolf, 7–8.

13. *Kemptville Advance*, 6 June 1895. Rutherford had "filled most of the important offices" in Court Kemptville, I.O.F., No. 214, and was a past master workman in the A.O.U.W. of Kemptville.

14. *South Edmonton News*, 20 June 1895.

15. *Edmonton Journal*, 14 May 1929.

16. *South Edmonton News*, 13 June 1895.

17. *Edmonton Journal*, 14 May 1929.

18. *South Edmonton News*, 13 December 1894. In a census taken the following spring, the population of South Edmonton had dropped to 505. Ibid., 2 May 1895.

19. Ibid., 8 November 1894.

20. Marzolf, 8.

21. R. C. Brown and R. Cook, *Canada 1896–1921, A Nation Transformed* (Toronto: McClelland and Stewart, 1974), 50.

22. Canada Census, 1891, 1901.

23. L. H. Thomas, *The Struggle for Responsible Government in the Northwest Territories 1870–97* (Toronto: University of Toronto Press, 1978), 104.

24. All but two of Alberta's first seven premiers were Ontario-born. The exceptions, Premiers Greenfield and Reid, were Britons. E. C. Manning became the first prairie-born premier in 1943, replacing Ontario-born William Aberhart.

25. Thomas, 151.

26. D. R. Owram, ed., *The Formation of Alberta: A Documentary History* (Calgary: Historical Society of Alberta, 1979), 82.

27. Ibid., 89–90.

28. Lots 25, 26, 27, and 28, block 1, river lot 13. K. Mather, *Rutherford House* (Edmonton: Parks and Recreation Report, 1973), 11. The house address later became 8715 - 104 Street.

29. The house measured 30 ft 6 in (9.3 m) x 26 ft 7 in (8.1 m), the kitchen 12 ft (3.7 m) x 24 ft (7.3 m). Ibid., 11.

30. Ibid., passim. The original Rutherford House was moved to Fort Edmonton Park in July 1968, where it has been restored as a feature of the 1905 street.

31. *South Edmonton News*, 17 October 1895.

32. *Alberta Plaindealer*, 25 November 1898.

33. Ibid., 30 June 1899.

34. *South Edmonton News*, 9 July 1896.

35. Ibid., 30 July 1896.

36. Ibid., 6 August 1896.

37. *Alberta Plaindealer*, 14 October 1898.

38. Ibid., 11 November 1898.

39. *Edmonton Bulletin*, 13 January 1897.

40. *Alberta Plaindealer*, 17 March 1898. The crown prosecutor in this case was N. D. Beck, Q.C., later a member of the royal commission that investigated Rutherford's role in the Alberta and Great Waterways agreement.

41. Marzolf, 9.

42. *Alberta Plaindealer*, 4 August 1899.

43. *South Edmonton News*, 11 March 1897.

44. Ibid., 28 October 1898. Rutherford was a director and secretary-treasurer of the Star Mining Co., which operated a dredge on the North Saskatchewan River. Ibid., 27 January 1898.

45. *Alberta Plaindealer*, 13 October 1899.

46. Personal communication, Mrs. Hazel McCuaig.

47. *Alberta Plaindealer*, 8 December 1899.

48. Ibid., 9 May 1902.

49. Ibid.

50. Ibid., 16 May 1902.

51. Ibid., 23 May 1902.

52. Ibid., 26 June 1903; and 21 October 1904.

53. Ibid., 9 January 1903.

54. Ibid., 3 April 1903.

55. Ibid., 22 January 1904.

56. Ibid., 21 February 1902.

57. Ibid., 17 July 1903.

58. Ibid., 8 January 1904.

59. Socially prominent women were "at home," prepared to receive visitors on specified days of the month. Mrs. Hazel McCuaig recalls that Mrs. Rutherford was "at home" on the fourth Monday of each month.

60. Ibid., 18 April 1902.

61. Ibid., 27 January 1905.

62. L. G. Thomas, *The Liberal Party in Alberta* (Toronto: University of Toronto Press, 1959), 16.

63. *Alberta Plaindealer*, 27 January 1905.

64. Ibid., 10 February 1905.

65. L. G. Thomas, 19.

66. Ibid., 16.

67. *Alberta Plaindealer*, 11 August 1905.

68. Owram, 370–71.

69. Ibid., 368–69.

70. *Alberta Plaindealer*, 11 August 1905.

Chapter II – Include inclusive text page numbers

1. *Strathcona Plaindealer*, 8 September 1905.

2. Ibid., 1 September 1905.

3. Ibid., 25 August 1905.

4. Ibid., 1 September 1905.

5. Ibid., 8 September 1905.

6. L. G. Thomas, *The Liberal Party in Alberta* (Toronto: University of Toronto Press, 1959), 22.

7. *Strathcona Plaindealer*, 8 September 1905.

8. John Blue, *Alberta Past and Present* (Chicago: Pioneer Historical Publishing Co., 1924), 1: 143–44.

9. L. G. Thomas, 30.

10. *Strathcona Plaindealer*, 10 November 1905. Cecil Rutherford, absent at Woodstock College, missed the event.

11. Ibid., 8 September 1905.

12. Thistle Rink, constructed in 1902, was located on the southeast corner of 102 Street and 102 Avenue. It burned to the ground on the night of 30 October 1913.

13. McKay Avenue School still stands at 10425 - 99 Avenue.

14. Located on the southwest corner of 106 Street and 96 Avenue, the original Terrace Building was demolished in 1961.

15. Rutherford Papers, U.A.A., Chipman to Rutherford, 11 July 1906; Strathcona to Rutherford, 10 October 1906; and A.D. Marzolf, "Alexander Cameron Rutherford

and his influence on Alberta's Educational Program" (M.Ed. thesis, University of Alberta, 1961), 5.

16. *Canadian Annual Review of Public Affairs* (hereafter cited as C.A.R.) (Toronto: Canadian Annual Review Publishing Co. Ltd., 1906), 472, 476.

17. Ibid., 1906–1909, passim.

18. L. G. Thomas, 53.

19. Ibid., 42.

20. *C.A.R.*, 1906–1909, passim.

21. Ibid., 1908, 511.

22. Marzolf, 68–70.

23. *C.A.R.*, 1908, 512.

24. *Edmonton Journal*, 14 May 1929.

25. Rutherford Papers, U.A.A., Laurier to Rutherford, 29 March 1907.

26. *Edmonton Journal*, 14 May 1929. More than thirty years later, W. M.Davidson, writing in the *Calgary Albertan* (23 August 1941) described Rutherford's decision in favour of Strathcona as "the despotic act of a small dictator. That one selfish act not only aroused the bitterest disappointment to Calgarians, but it turned out to be a disastrous blow to the government. [People] . . . learned the stature of the premier who had stepped down from his pinnacle and revealed himself in his real parochialism."

27. *C.A.R.*, 1906, 472, 476.

28. Rutherford Papers, U.A.A., Government of Alberta Telephone Service, 1908.

29. *Strathcona Plaindealer*, 8 January 1909.

30. Rutherford Papers, U.A.A., Talbot to Rutherford, 12 June 1908.

31. *C.A.R.*, 1909, 551.

32. L. G. Thomas, 57.

33. Despite his farm background, Rutherford never learned to handle horses either. Before he bought his car, he was dependent on friends for transportation. W. H. Wilkin was his most constant driver. The two lawyers were a familiar sight commuting across the Saskatchewan River by buggy at the ford at Walterdale Flats. Both men would hoist their feet onto the dashboard of the buggy just before the horse splashed into the river. E. Stewart-Richmond, "A Firm Foundation," in *Alberta Writers Speak* (Edmonton: Words Unlimited Writers Group, 1969), 38.

34. L. G. Thomas, 58–59.

35. *Strathcona Chronicle*, 27 November 1908.

36. L. G. Thomas, 62–63; and *C.A.R.*, 1910, 553–554.

37. Marzolf, 44.

38. *Strathcona Plaindealer*, 5 March 1909.

39. Ibid., 16 March 1909.

40. L. G. Thomas, 68.

41. *Strathcona Plaindealer*, 19 March 1909.

42. L. G. Thomas, 69. Michener's son, Roland, was later to become governor-general of Canada.

43. *Strathcona Plaindealer*, 23 March 1909.

44. Ibid., 19 October 1906.

45. *C.A.R.*, 1907, 311.

46. Personal communication, Mrs. Hazel McCuaig.

47. *Strathcona Plaindealer*, 22 November 1907.

48. Marzolf, 42.

49. *Strathcona Plaindealer*, 2 February 1909.

50. Ibid., 3 July 1908.

51. Ibid., 17 August 1909.

52. Ibid., 8 October 1907.

53. Ibid., 14 October 1908. Constructed in 1905 - 1906, enlarged in 1912, and renamed Queen Alexandra School, the building still stands at 7730 - 106 Street.

54. Ibid., 20 March 1908.

55. Ibid., 31 March 1908.

56. Ibid., 25 September 1908.

57. Rutherford Papers, U.A.A., University Library Correspondence.

58. *Strathcona Plaindealer*, 22 October 1907. Now called the Old Scona Academic High School, the former collegiate still stands at 10523 - 84 Avenue.

59. Ibid., 4 January 1910.

60. *Edmonton Journal*, 10 September 1955.

61. Rutherford Papers, U.A.A., Strathcona to Rutherford, 10 October 1906.

62. *Strathcona Plaindealer*, 31 December 1907. The legislative building was designed by Provincial Architect (1907–1912) Allan M. Jeffers, a graduate of the Rhode Island School of Design in the United States.

63. Ibid., 5 October 1909.

64. Ibid., 17 November, 1 December 1908.

65. Ibid., 10 December 1907.

66. Ibid., 7 September 1906.

67. Ibid., 2 October 1906.

68. Ibid., 29 September 1908.

69. Ibid., 29 January 1909.

70. Ibid., 12 April 1910.

71. The University Women's Club would later play a key role in the struggle to save Rutherford House.

72. Ibid., 12 May 1908.

73. Personal communication, Mrs. Hazel McCuaig.

74. *Strathcona Plaindealer*, 4 September 1908.

75. Ibid., 22 February 1907.

76. Ibid., 7 May 1907.

77. Ibid., 10 May 1907.

78. Ibid., 31 May, 1 July 1907. The Royal Bank of Canada building, constructed c. 1913, now stands on the site of the Rutherford Block.

79. Ibid., 3 July 1908.

80. Personal communication, Mrs. Hazel McCuaig.

81. *Strathcona Plaindealer*, 30 April 1907.

82. Rutherford Papers, U.A.A., Rutherford to *Halifax Morning Chronicle*, 28 December 1906.

Chapter III – Include inclusive text page numbers

1. A. D. Marzolf, "Alexander Cameron Rutherford and his Influence on Alberta's Educational Program" (M. Ed. thesis, University of Alberta, 1961), 121–22.

2. *Strathcona Plaindealer*, 22 October 1909.

3. Rutherford Papers, U.A.A., Cushing to Rutherford, 5 February 1910.

4. Ibid., Boyle to Rutherford, 18 June 1909.

5. *Strathcona Plaindealer*, 18 February 1910.

6. Rutherford Papers, U.A.A., W. H. Cushing, January 1910.

7. L. G. Thomas, *The Liberal Party in Alberta* (Toronto: University of Toronto Press, 1959), 61.

8. Rutherford Papers, U.A.A., A. & G.W. Railway.

9. *Strathcona Plaindealer*, 18 February 1910.

10. Ibid., 22 February 1910.

11. Ibid.

12. Ibid.

13. Ibid., 4 March 1910.

14. L. G. Thomas, 79.

15. Ibid., 80.

16. Ibid., 82.

17. Ibid., 85.

18. Rutherford Papers, U.A.A., Rutherford to Ingram, 4 April 1910.

19. L. G. Thomas, 87.

20. Ibid., 88.

21. Marzolf, 50.

22. L. G. Thomas, 91.

23. Royal Commission on the A. & G.W. Railway. Report (Edmonton, 1910), 4.

24. Ibid., 37–38.

25. Ibid., 34–38.

26. Ibid., 57.

27. John Blue concluded, for example, "The majority report considered the government as mildly censurable in some of its arrangements and actions, but *completely exonerated* [emphasis added] Premier Rutherford and Attorney-General Cross from having any personal interest in the scheme or negotiations." Blue, *Alberta Past and Present* (Chicago: Pioneer Historical Publishing Co., 1924), 1: 127.

28. *Edmonton Journal*, 11 November 1910.

29. Ibid.

30. *Edmonton Capital* and *Edmonton Journal*, 15 December 1910.

31. L. G. Thomas, 131.

32. *Strathcona Plaindealer*, 11 August 1905.

33. W. A. Griesbach, *I Remember* (Toronto: Ryerson Press, 1946), 332.

34. Marzolf, 51.

35. E. A. Corbett, *Henry Marshall Tory* (Toronto: Ryerson Press, 1954), 104.

36. Personal communication, Mrs. Hazel McCuaig.

37. Rutherford Papers, Provincial Archives of Alberta (hereafter cited as P.A.A.), 75.518/23.

38. Ibid., 75.518/24.

Chapter IV – Include inclusive text page numbers

1. L. G. Thomas, *The Liberal Party in Alberta* (Toronto: University of Toronto Press, 1959), 96.

2. Ibid., 112.

3. *Edmonton Capital*, 22, 23 November, 6 December 1910.

4. Rutherford Papers, U.A.A., Cross to Rutherford, 23 August 1910.

5. Mrs. Hazel McCuaig recalls that Mrs. Rutherford hoped her husband would get a senate appointment in 1905 instead of the premiership; it would have been a less taxing career and would have taken them back to Ottawa, which she missed very deeply.

6. Law Society of Alberta, Roll 20: Alexander Cameron Rutherford.

7. L. G. Thomas, 30.

8. *Strathcona Plaindealer*, 7 October 1910.

9. Ibid., 11 October 1910. The enlarged elementary school still stands at 8620 - 91 Street.

10. Ibid., 15 November 1910.

11. *Edmonton Bulletin*, 6 February 1911. A.D. Marzolf, ("Alexander Cameron Rutherford and his Influence on Alberta's Educational Program," M. Ed. thesis, University of Alberta, 1961, 10) and others give the date as 22 May 1911, but the earlier date is supported by an entry in the 18 April issue of the *Strathcona Plaindealer*, reporting that Dr. A. McPherson and family had moved into the residence lately occupied by Hon. Dr. Rutherford.

12. *Strathcona Plaindealer*, 10 March 1911.

13. While he was in London, Rutherford was photographed in the studio of Elliott and Fry, 55 Baker Street. This full-length portrait apparently inspired two paintings of Rutherford, one of which now hangs in the legislative building. The original Elliott and Fry portrait is now in the custody of Historic Sites Service, Alberta Culture and Multiculturalism.

14. *Strathcona Plaindealer*, 21 April 1911.

15. L. G. Thomas, 132.

16. *Strathcona Plaindealer*, 18 August 1911.

17. *Edmonton Capital*, 17 August 1911.

18. L. G. Thomas, 120.

19. *Strathcona Plaindealer*, 15 August 1911.

20. Ibid., 22 August 1911.

21. L. G. Thomas, 120.

22. *Strathcona Plaindealer*, 29 August 1911.

23. *Edmonton Capital*, 29 August 1911.

24. Ibid., 6 September 1911.

25. L. G. Thomas, 122–23.

26. Ibid., 129.

27. *Edmonton Bulletin*, 27 March 1913.

28. Ibid., 31 March 1913. Strathcona had amalgamated with Edmonton the year before.

29. Ibid., *sic.*

30. Ibid., 1 April 1913, *sic.*

31. *Edmonton Journal*, 1 April 1913.

32. Ibid., 1 April, 3 April 1913.

33. Ibid., 18 April 1913.

34. *Edmonton Journal*, 7 July 1921.

35. Ibid., 11 July 1921.

36. Ibid., 12 July 1921.

37. Alwyn Bramley-Moore, *Canada and Her Colonies or Home Rule for Alberta* (London: W. Stewart and Co., 1911). Bramley-Moore (1878–1916) was born in London, England and emigrated to Ontario in 1898. In 1903 he settled at Lloydminster, District of Saskatchewan, N.W.T., where he won election to the second Alberta Legislature in 1909. He died in France in April 1916 while serving with the Princess Patricia's Canadian Light Infantry in World War I.

38. Ibid., 47–48.

39. Ibid., ix.

40. Ibid., 150.

41. Ibid., 171.

42. Not surprisingly, Rutherford privately expressed considerable sympathy for the United Farmers of Alberta government. Personal communication, Mr. and Mrs. S. H. McCuaig, 8 February 1979.

Chapter V – Include inclusive text page numbers

1. *Strathcona Plaindealer*, 24 September 1909.

2. Ibid., 11 November 1910.

3. The Imperial Bank Building at 10319 Whyte Avenue, later (1949) the Bank of Nova Scotia, was demolished in 1963 or 1964, according to the *Henderson Directory*.

4. *Alberta Law Report*, Vol. XI, 395 and Vol. XV, 194–96.

5. *Alberta Law Reports, Dominion Law Reports, Western Weekly Reports*, 1910–40.

6. *Strathcona Plaindealer*, 4 April 1911; and personal communication, Mrs. Hazel McCuaig.

7. Personal communication, Mrs. Hazel McCuaig.

8. Personal communication, University Art Gallery.

9. *Edmonton Bulletin*, 12 June 1941.

10. *The Trail*, No. 19 (May 1927): 2.

11. *Strathcona Plaindealer*, 10 May 1912.

12. *Edmonton Journal*, 10 May 1938.

13. Ibid., 23 May 1927. According to the *Edmonton Bulletin* (23 May 1927) the election took place on May 20.

14. Copy from the personal papers of Mrs. Helen Rutherford. Mrs. Rutherford remembered hearing Dr. Rutherford repeat these words aloud in his bedroom the night before the 1941 convocation, when he was living with Cecil Rutherford and herself.

15. *Edmonton Journal*, 10 September 1955. During his fourteen years as chancellor, Dr. Rutherford missed only the 1940 convocation, when he was too ill to attend.

16. Personal communication, Mrs. Helen Rutherford. Because he was nearsighted, Dr. Rutherford removed his glasses to read.

17. Mrs. Hazel McCuaig, quoted in the *Edmonton Journal*, 10 September 1955.

18. Dr. R. C. Wallace, Address at the opening of the Rutherford Library, 15 May 1951. *New Trail* 9 (2):76, quoted in *News from the Rare Book Room* 2 (3): 4.

19. *News from the Rare Book Room* 2 (3): 5.

20. Minutes, Board of Governors, University of Alberta, 21 March 1950.

21. J. S. Nicks, "Rutherford House: Edmonton, Alberta" (Manuscript, Historic Sites Service, Alberta Culture and Multiculturalism, Edmonton 1970), 6.

22. A. O. MacRae, *The History of the Province of Alberta* (Calgary: Western Canada History Co., 1912), 495.

23. John Blue, *Alberta Past and Present* (Chicago: Pioneer Historical Publishing Co., 1924), 2: 5.

24. Rutherford Papers, U.A.A., Business Matters.

25. Personal communication, Catherine Cooper Cole, G.W.G. historian; *The Great Western Garment Company: The First Seventy-Five Years* (Anniversary commemorative booklet, 1986); and *Edmonton Journal*, 1 November 1986.

26. *The Canadian Law Lists* (Hardy's), Law Library, University of Alberta; and *Edmonton Bulletin*, 18 September 1919.

27. Records of Strathcona Baptist Church, courtesy of Mr. J. Williams.

28. Historical notes, courtesy of Mrs. Hazel McCuaig.

29. Charles E. Redeker, "Early History of the Benevolent and Protective Order of Elks of the Dominion of Canada and Newfoundland" (Manuscript, Windsor, Ontario, 1937. Copy on file, Historic Sites Service, Alberta Culture and Multiculturalism, Edmonton).

30. Historical notes, courtesy of Mrs. Hazel McCuaig.

31. Blue, 2: 6.

32. Ibid.

33. *Edmonton Bulletin*, 27 May 1916. The colours now hang in the rotunda of the Legislative Building in Edmonton.

34. Nicks, 6.

35. *Alberta Historical Review* 5 (4): 29.

36. Cecil E. Denny, *The Law Marches West* (Toronto: J.M. Dent and Sons, 1939), ix–x.

37. Historical notes, courtesy of Mrs. Hazel McCuaig.

38. Edmonton Branch C.A.A. to Cecil Rutherford, 12 June 1941, courtesy of Mrs. Helen Rutherford.

39. *Edmonton Journal*, 20 December 1938.

40. Blue, 2: 6.

41. A. D. Marzolf, "Alexander Cameron Rutherford and his Influence on Alberta's Educational Program" (M. Ed. Thesis, University of Alberta, 1961), 18. Dr. Broadus was the first (1908) professor of English at the University of Alberta and a close friend of Dr. Rutherford's.

42. Historical notes, courtesy of Mrs. Hazel McCuaig.

43. *Edmonton Journal*, 20 December 1938.

44. Minutes of the Mayfair Golf and Country Club 1920, courtesy of L.A.W. Blindenbach, general manager.

45. Personal communication, Lorri Storr from Mrs. Ruth Bate.

46. E. Stewart-Richmond, "A Firm Foundation," in *Alberta Writers Speak* (Edmonton: Words Unlimited Writers Group, 1969), 40.

47. John Campbell Bowen was lieutenant-governor of Alberta from 1937 to 1950.

48. *Edmonton Bulletin*, 12 June 1941.

49. Walter H. Johns, *A History of the University of Alberta 1908–1969* (Edmonton: University of Alberta Press, 1981), 162–170.

50. Ibid., 165.

Chapter VI – Include inclusive text page numbers

1. The Plan of Edmonton Settlement, N.W.T., Department of the Interior, Dominion Lands Office, 1883, Land Titles Office, Edmonton. Surveyed by M. Deane D.L.S. in 1882, the plan shows Laurence Garneau in possession of river lot 7 opposite Fort Edmonton. Garneau was issued a certificate of ownership (286 B) on 12 May 1888 in fee simple for river lot 7, an estate of 234.88 acres (95.1 hectares). In 1891 Garneau began disposing of a number of 1- and 2-acre (0.4- and 0.8-hectare) parcels from his estate (Certificates of Title 36 O, 142 Q, 390 I, 188 T 1, 201 Z 1, 206 E 2, 207 E 2, 190 Q 2, 191 Q 2, and others) and turned over a large acreage on the east side of his estate to the Catholic church.

2. Plan 443 X, being a subdivision of part of river lot 7, surveyed by Robert W. Lendrum D.L.S. and registered on 28 April 1909, Land Titles Office, Edmonton.

3. Certificate of Title 3F 10, Land Titles Office, Edmonton.

4. *Strathcona Plaindealer*, 9 October 1908. Arthur G. Wilson and D.Easton Herrald designed many public buildings and residences in Strathcona, including the fire station, the city hall, the library, and the university hospital. H. J. Boam, *Twentieth Century Impressions of Canada* (Montreal: Sells Ltd., 1914), 721.

5. *Strathcona Plaindealer*, 2 November 1909.

6. *Edmonton Bulletin*, 18 May 1910.

7. Personal communication, Mrs. Hazel McCuaig.

8. U.A.A., Acc. No. 76-25-338.

9. The Rutherfords used this barn for a Jersey cow they kept for a few years until the barn was destroyed by fire. The cow substituted for milk delivery during the pre–World War I years, before milk wagons reached this part of the community. It was one of the duties of the Rutherford maids to milk the cow and bring home the milk, but Mrs. Rutherford also learned to milk the cow. Personal communication, Mrs. Hazel McCuaig.

10. Ibid.

11. L. G. Thomas, "The Rutherford House and its place in Alberta architecture," *New Trail* (Winter 1966–67): 6.

12. Ibid., 7.

13. Personal communication, Mrs. Hazel McCuaig.

14. An engagement ring, thrown down during a lovers' quarrel, was found in the summer house in the early 1920s. Happily, the couple were later re-united, but the finder, a girl looking after the McCuaig children, kept the ring. Ibid.

15. The vegetable garden was located west of the house and was large enough for a few neighbours to have plots in it. Ibid.

16. Ibid.

17. Ibid.

18. Mrs. Hazel McCuaig remembers that the original fireplace in the library was electric but was converted to gas when the electric elements ("bulbs") became scarce. L. G. Thomas ("Rutherford House," 6) also reports an electric heater in the library fireplace, "placed there to keep the books dry." On the other hand, Bob Anderson, architect in charge of the Rutherford House restoration, could find no evidence of an electrical outlet in the fireplace and believes that it was originally an open fireplace before being converted to gas. Anderson's position is supported by a desciption of a tea at Rutherford House in the *Strathcona Plaindealer* (7 November 1911): "The library, with its books and big bright fire attracted many guests. . . ."

19. L. G. Thomas ("Rutherford House," 6) reports a double inglenook, and Mrs. Helen Rutherford also remembers an inglenook on each side of the fireplace, the one on the left with a high back that partially blocked the fireplace area from the hall entrance to the breakfast room.

20. Mrs. Hazel McCuaig recalls that the narrow window in the den originally held stained glass.

21. Personal communication, Mrs. Hazel McCuaig.

22. Personal communication, Bob Anderson.

23. Personal communication, Mrs. Hazel McCuaig.

24. *Edmonton Journal*, 14 May 1929; and L. R. Muirhead, ed., *Scotland* (London: E. Benn, 1959), 361–62.

25. *Edmonton Journal*, 22 October 1957.

26. *Edmonton Bulletin*, 18 September 1919.

27. Personal communication, Mrs. Hazel McCuaig.

28. Ibid.

29. On 13 May 1924 Certificate of Title No. 15U59 was registered in the name of Hazel R. McCuaig for a 50 ft x 91 ft lot in the southwest corner of lot 12. Land Titles Office, Edmonton.

30. Apparently many maids lived at Rutherford House between 1911 and 1940. Some of them were young German or other immigrant women. The turnover was fairly rapid in the early years, perhaps because of the relative isolation of the house, but later maids stayed for a year or more. During Mrs. Rutherford's final years, when she was unable to prepare meals, housekeepers lived in the house.

31. The McCuaig children seem to have spent as much time at their grandparents' as at home, and were not above pillow fighting in the library or sliding down the bannisters. Personal communication, Mrs. Hazel McCuaig.

32. Plan 3637 E.T., surveyed by Reginald H. Coutley A.L.S. on 23–24 April 1928, approved 9 July 1928, Land Titles Office, Edmonton.

33. *Edmonton Journal*, 13 September 1940.

34. Personal communication, Mrs. Hazel McCuaig.

35. *Strathcona Plaindealer*, 5 September 1911. The Rutherford piano, which was played by both Mrs. Rutherford and Hazel, stood in the parlour, variously called the drawing room or the music room.

36. Ibid., 7 November 1911. Some of Mrs. Rutherford's gowns were ordered from Paris. Personal communication, Mrs. Ruth Bate.

37. Ibid., 29 November 1911.

38. Ibid., 9 April 1912.

39. Ibid., 12 July 1912.

40. Ibid., 26 January, 3 February 1912.

41. Ibid., 10 May 1912.

42. *Edmonton Journal*, 10 May 1938.

43. Personal communication, Mrs. Hazel McCuaig.

44. *The Trail*, No. 19 (May 1927): 2.

45. *Edmonton Journal*, 10 May 1938.

46. Ibid., 10 May 1935.

47. *Edmonton Bulletin*, 10 May 1931. William L. Walsh was lieutenant-governor of Alberta from 1931 to 1936.

48. L.G. Thomas, "Rutherford House," 5.

49. The Paul James Papers, Glenbow Archives, 11 July 1920.

50. Personal communication, Mrs. Hazel McCuaig.

51. Personal communication, Mrs. Helen Rutherford.

52. Personal communication, Mrs. Hazel McCuaig.

53. *Alberta Historical Review* 4 (4): 29.

54. *Edmonton Journal*, 20 December 1938. Mrs. Rutherford was a Methodist and was never received into the Baptist church, but she attended the Strathcona Baptist Church with her husband and was socially active with its members. Mrs. Rutherford was a member of the Strathcona Methodist (later Metropolitan United) Church.

55. *Edmonton Bulletin*, 18 September 1919.

56. Arthur Miller in his late eighties still well remembered 19 December 1938. Miller was a piper with the 194th Battalion C.E.F., and was present in 1916 when Honorary Colonel A. C. Rutherford presented the colours to his battalion prior to its going overseas.

57. *Edmonton Bulletin*, 20 December 1938.

58. *Edmonton Journal*, 20 December 1938.

59. Ibid.

60. Personal communication, Mrs. Helen Rutherford.

61. Personal communication, Mrs. Hazel McCuaig.

62. Personal communication, Eric McCuaig, January 1989.

63. *Edmonton Bulletin*, 6 August 1900; and *Strathcona Plaindealer*, 15 August 1902.

64. Personal communication, Mrs. Hazel McCuaig.

65. *Edmonton Bulletin*, 16 September 1940.

66. Personal communication, Mrs. Hazel McCuaig.

67. *Edmonton Journal*, 13 May 1974.

68. S. H. McCuaig to Mayor V. M. Dantzer and the Edmonton City Commissioners, 1 March 1966. Copy courtesy of Mrs. Hazel McCuaig.

69. Ibid.; and S. H. McCuaig to Dr. Walter Johns, President of the University of Alberta, 1 March 1966. Copy courtesy of Mrs. Hazel McCuaig.

70. Historic Sites and Monuments Board of Canada, Agenda Paper 1966-35, 3 May 1966. Copy courtesy of Mrs. Lila Fahlman.

71. *Edmonton Journal*, 24 November 1966.

72. Ibid., 25 November 1966.

73. Personal communication, E. R. Shedden, University of Alberta, Campus Planning and Development.

74. *Edmonton Journal*, 19 March 1969.

75. University Women's Club of Edmonton to Chairman, University of Alberta Board of Governors, 25 April 1969. Copy courtesy of Mrs. Lila Fahlman.

76. E. R. Shedden, Campus Planning and Development, to the Society for the Preservation of Historical Homes, et al., 16 October 1969. Copy courtesy of Mrs. Lila Fahlman.

77. *Edmonton Journal*, 17 March 1967.

78. J. S. Nicks, "Rutherford House: Edmonton, Alberta" (Manuscript, Historic Sites Service, Alberta Culture and Multiculturalism, Edmonton 1970).

79. Personal communication, Bob Anderson.

80. *Edmonton Journal*, 17 November 1970.

81. Personal communication, Bob Anderson.

82. The following details regarding the restoration of Rutherford House were gathered from personal communication with Bob Anderson and from his 1971 interim report, "Rutherford House, Edmonton. Renovation and Restoration Report, No. 2," copy on file, Historic Sites Service, Alberta Culture and Multiculturalism, Edmonton.

83. The partition between the water closet and the storage room in the southwest corner was thickened about eight inches (twenty centimetres) at the expense of the storage room in order to accommodate a recessed wash basin in the water closet.

84. Report on Proposed Use of Rutherford House, B. A. McCorquodale, Provincial Museum of Alberta, 20 July 1972.

85. Personal communication, Bob Anderson.

86. Visitor register, Rutherford House, 1.

87. *Edmonton Journal*, 13 May 1974.

Epilogue – Include inclusive text page numbers

1. A. D. Marzolf, "Alexander Cameron Rutherford and his Influence on Alberta's Educational Program" (M. Ed. Thesis, University of Alberta, 1961), 1–2.

2. L. G. Thomas, *The Liberal Party in Alberta* (Toronto: University of Toronto Press, 1959).

3. Dr. R. C. Wallace, Address at the opening of the Rutherford Library, 15 May 1951. *New Trail* 9 (2): 76, quoted in *News From the Rare Book Room* 2 (3): 4.

4. *The Alberta Gazette*, 15 December 1954, 2026. Mount Rutherford is located in Jasper National Park at lat. 53° 10', long. 118° 25', three kilometres northeast of Harvey Lake.

5. Other Alberta pioneers who were so honoured at the time included H. M. Tory, Chief Justice H. Harvey, Frank Oliver, W. A. Griesbach, and F. W. G. Haultain, all of whom were associated with Dr. Rutherford's political career.

6. Presidential correspondence in reference to an honorary degree for Mrs. Hazel McCuaig, U.A.A., 26 May 1964. Mrs. Ruth Bowen, who prepared the citation in consultation with Mrs. Hazel McCuaig, delivered the citation at the spring 1964 Convocation.

7. Bruce Peel to Mrs. S. H. McCuaig, 29 December 1970, U.A.A.

8. *Winchester Press*, 27 November 1985.

9. Marzolf, 106– 8.

10. *Edmonton Journal*, 14 May 1929.

11. "Who's Who Out West," *Saturday Night*, 5 October 1907, 17.

12. "Premier A. C. Rutherford" (Biographical sketch, author unknown, Legislative Library, Old Timers File, 1908).

13. L. G. Thomas, National Heritage Day address at Rutherford House, 16 February 1987.

14. *Edmonton Journal*, 12 June 1941.

15. Personal communication, Mrs. Hazel McCuaig.

16. *Edmonton Journal*, 12 June 1941.

17. Chief Justice H. Harvey was co-author of the majority *Report* of the Royal Commission on the Alberta and Great Waterways Railway, 1910.

18. Donald E. Cameron, Funeral oration for Dr. A. C. Rutherford, Strathcona Baptist Church, 13 June 1941. Transcript courtesy of Mrs. Hazel McCuaig.

BIBLIOGRAPHY

I. Books

Blue, John. *Alberta Past and Present.* 3 vols. Chicago: Pioneer Historical Publishing Co., 1924.

Boam, H. J. *Twentieth Century Impressions of Canada.* Montreal: Sells Ltd., 1914.

Bramley-Moore, Alwyn. *Canada and Her Colonies or Home Rule for Alberta.* London: W. Stewart and Co., 1911.

Brown, R.C. and Cook, R. *Canada 1896–1921, A Nation Transformed.* Toronto: McClelland and Stewart, 1974.

Corbett, E. A. *Henry Marshall Tory, Beloved Canadian.* Toronto: Ryerson Press, 1954.

Denny, Cecil E. *The Law Marches West.* Toronto: J.M. Dent and Sons, 1939.

Griesbach, W. A. *I Remember.* Toronto: Ryerson Press, 1946.

Johns, Walter H. *A History of the University of Alberta 1908–1969.* Edmonton: University of Alberta Press, 1981.

Macdonald, John. *The History of the University of Alberta, 1908–1958.* Toronto: W. J. Gage, 1958.

MacRae, A. O. *The History of the Province of Alberta.* Calgary: Western Canada History Co., 1912.

Muirhead, L. Russell, ed. *Scotland.* London: Ernest Benn Ltd., 1959.

Owram, D.R., ed. *The Formation of Alberta: A Documentary History.* Calgary: Historical Society of Alberta, 1979.

Rutherford, Helen Martin. "Inside Rutherford House." In *Strathcona Harvest*, edited by Elsie Park Gowan, 29–32. Edmonton: Spartan Press Ltd., 1974.

Stewart-Richmond, E. "A Firm Foundation." In *Alberta Writers Speak*, 36–40. Edmonton: Words Unlimited Writers Group, 1969.

Thomas, L. G. *The Liberal Party in Alberta.* Toronto: University of Toronto Press, 1959.

Thomas, L. H. *The Struggle for Responsible Government in the Northwest Territories 1870–97.* Toronto: University of Toronto Press, 1978.

II. Periodicals

"Alexander Cameron Rutherford, 1858–1941." *Alberta Historical Review* 4: 29.

Canadian Law Lists (Hardy's). Agincourt, Ontario: 1910–1940.

Clark, D., Bodnar, D., Pasnak, J. "Architectural Heritage." *Canadian Collector,* January–February 1976, 57–62.

Hamilton, Dorothy I. "The Dr. A. C. Rutherford Canadiana Collection, Part 1." University of Alberta. *News from the Rare Book Room* 2: 1–6.

Hopkins, J. Castell, ed. *Canadian Annual Review of Public Affairs.* Toronto: Canadian Annual Review Publishing Co. Ltd., 1905–1911.

Kerr, W. A. R. "Hon. A. C. Rutherford, K. C., LL.D." University of Alberta. *Evergreen and Gold* 8 (1928): 7.

"The U. of A.'s New Chancellor." *The Trail* 19 (May 1927): 1–2.

Thomas, L. G. "The Liberal Party in Alberta." *Canadian Historical Review* 27 (1947): 411–427.

_____. "The Rutherford House and its place in Alberta architecture." *New Trail* (Winter 1966–67): 5–7.

Dr. A. C. Wallace. Address at opening of Rutherford Library. *New Trail* 9 (2): 76–78.

"Who's Who out West." *Saturday Night* , 5 October 1907, 17.

III. Unpublished Material

Anderson, Bob. "Rutherford House, Edmonton. Renovation and Restoration Report No. 2." Report on file Historic Sites Service, Alberta Culture and Multiculturalism, Edmonton, n.d.

Marzolf, Archie D. "Alexander Cameron Rutherford and his Influence on Alberta's Educational Program." M.Ed. thesis, University of Alberta, 1961.

Mather, Ken. "Rutherford House." Report on file Historical Section, Edmonton Parks and Recreation: 1973.

Nicks, John. "Rutherford House, Edmonton, Alberta." Report on file Historic Sites Service, Alberta Culture and Multiculturalism, Edmonton: 1970.

Redeker, Charles E. "Early History of the Benevolent and Protective Order of Elks of the Dominion of Canada and Newfoundland." Manuscript, Windsor, Ontario,

1937. Copy on file Historic Sites Service, Alberta Culture and Multiculturalism, Edmonton.

IV. Government Documents

Alberta. Royal Commission on the Alberta and Great Waterways Railway Co. *Report*. Edmonton, 1910. On file Legislature Library, Edmonton.

The Alberta Gazette. December 15, 1954.

V. Manuscript Collections

Calgary, Alberta. Glenbow-Alberta Institute. Paul James Papers.

Edmonton, Alberta. University of Alberta Archives. Minutes of the University Board of Governors.

Edmonton, Alberta. Provincial Archives of Alberta. Rutherford Papers.

Edmonton, Alberta. University of Alberta Archives. Rutherford Papers.

Edmonton, Alberta. James D. Williams, custodian. Scona Baptist Church Records.

VI. Interviews

Unless otherwise specified in the notes, all interviews were conducted at various dates during the years 1975 and 1976.

Anderson, Bob. Architect, Alberta Government Services, Edmonton, Alberta.

Bate, Ruth. Granddaughter of A. C. Rutherford, Edmonton, Alberta.

Blindenbach, L. A. W. General Manager, Mayfair Golf and Country Club, Edmonton, Alberta.

Collinson, Helen. Curator, University of Alberta Art Gallery, Edmonton, Alberta.

Fahlman, Lila. Past President, Society for the Preservation of Historic Homes, Edmonton, Alberta.

McCuaig, Eric. Grandson of A. C. Rutherford, Edmonton, Alberta.

McCuaig, Hazel. Daughter of A. C. Rutherford, Edmonton, Alberta.

McCuaig, Stanley. Son-in-law of A. C. Rutherford, Edmonton, Alberta.

Miller, Arthur. Former Piper, 194th Battalion, C.E.F., Edmonton, Alberta.

Rutherford, Helen. Daughter-in-law of A. C. Rutherford, Edmonton, Alberta.

Shedden, E. R. University of Alberta, Campus Planning and Development, Edmonton, Alberta.

VII. Newspapers

Alberta Plaindealer

Calgary Albertan

Edmonton Bulletin

Edmonton Journal

Kemptville Advance

South Edmonton News

Strathcona Chronicle

Strathcona Plaindealer

Winchester Press

INDEX

189